Rath & Strong's

SIX SIGMA
POCKET GUIDE

6σ

CONTROL · DEFINE · MEASURE · ANALYZE · IMPROVE

RATH & STRONG
Management Consultants
Founded in 1935

AON Management Consulting

Rath & Strong Management Consultants
45 Hayden Avenue
Suite 2700
Lexington, Massachusetts 02421
Tel: 781/861-1700
e-mail: rathstronginfo@aoncons.com
www.rathstrong.com

Dedication

Rath & Strong's Six Sigma Pocket Guide is dedicated to the memory of Dorian Shainin and Frank Satterthwaite, our late esteemed colleagues who pioneered industrial problem solving and statistical methodologies such as advanced diagnostic tools (ADT) and planned experimentation (PE). Their approaches were integral to the development of Pre-Control and Random Balance, techniques used to find causes of defects and measure variation, that later became key to Statistical Process Control and Six Sigma methodology.

Tool Name	Chapter Number and Page	Phase of DMAIC in which tool is most commonly used (Define, Measure, Analyze, Innovative Improvement, Control)				
		D	M	A	I	C
Affinity Diagram	2/15	●		●		
Brainstorming	4/96			●	●	
Business Case	2/8	●				
Cause-and-Effect Diagrams	4/99			●		
Charter	2/8	●				
Consensus	5/153				●	
Control Charts	3/62		●	●	●	●
For continuous data						
Individuals	3/62					
X-Bar, R	3/65					
EWMA	6/180					
For discrete data						
p, np	6/174					
c, u	6/176					
CTQ (Critical-to-Quality) Tree	2/18	●				
Data Collection Forms	3/37		●	●	●	●
Check Sheet	3/37					
Frequency Plot Check Sheet	3/38					
Confirmation Check Sheet	3/39					
Concentration Diagram	3/40					
Data Collection Plan	3/22		●	●	●	●
Design of Experiments	4/137			●	●	
Full Factorial	4/137					
Reduced Fractions	4/146					

Tool Name	Chapter Number and Page	Phase of DMAIC in which tool is most commonly used (Define, Measure, Analyze, Innovative Improvement, Control)				
		D	M	A	I	C
Design of Experiments *(Cont'd.)*						
Screening Designs	4/148					
Plackett-Burnham Designs	4/148					
More than Two Levels	4/149					
Flow Diagrams	4/104	●	●	●	●	●
Frequency Plots	3/70		●	●	●	●
FMEA *Failure Mode and Effect Analysis*	3/26		●		●	
Gage R & R	3/41		●			
Hypothesis Tests	4/118			●		
t-test	4/125					
Paired t-test	4/126					
ANOVA	4/127					
Chi Square	4/128					
Kano Model	2/17		●			
Planning Tools	5/158				●	
Gantt Charts	5/158					
Planning Grid	5/160					
Pareto Charts	3/83		●	●	●	
Prioritization Matrix	3/26		●		●	
Process Capability	3/86		●		●	
Process Sigma	3/88		●		●	
Quality Control Process Chart	6/164					●

Tool Name	Chapter Number and Page	Phase of DMAIC in which tool is most commonly used (Define, Measure, Analyze, Innovative Improvement, Control)				
		D	M	A	I	C
Regression	4/130			●		
Rolled Throughput Yield	2/12	●				
Sampling	3/47		●	●	●	●
Scatter Plots	4/115			●		
SIPOC	2/11	●				
Stakeholder Analysis	2/9	●			●	
Standardization	6/167					●
Stratification	3/32		●	●	●	●
Stratified Frequency Plots	4/111			●		
Time Series Plots (Run Charts)	3/57		●			
VOC (Voice of the Customer)	2/13	●				

DMAIC

DMAIC is an acronym meaning **D**efine, **M**easure, **A**nalyze, **I**mprove, **C**ontrol. It is a structured, disciplined, rigorous approach to process improvement consisting of the five phases mentioned, where each phase is linked logically to the previous phase as well as to the next phase. The reason to follow this rigorous methodology is to achieve the stretch goal of Six Sigma or 3.4 defects per million opportunities.

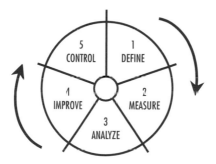

DEFINE

The first phase is **Define**. The project's purpose and scope are defined. Background information on the process and customer is collected. The output of this phase is:

1. A clear statement of the intended improvement (the business case and team charter)

2. A high-level map of the process (SIPOC)

3. A list of what is important to the customer(s)

This solid definition links to the next phase.

MEASURE

The goal of the **Measure** phase is to focus the improvement effort by gathering information on the current situation. The output of Measure is:

1. Baseline data on current process performance

2. Data that pinpoints problem location or occurrence

3. A more focused problem statement

These outputs will provide the basis for the next phase.

ANALYZE

The goal of the **Analyze** phase is to identify root cause(s) and confirm them with data. The output is a theory that has been tested and confirmed. The verified cause(s) will form the basis for solutions in the next phase.

IMPROVE

The goal of **Improve** phase is to try out and implement solutions that address root causes. The output is planned, tested actions that should eliminate or reduce the impact of the identified root cause(s). Additionally, a plan is created for how results will be evaluated in the next phase.

CONTROL

The goal of **Control** phase is to evaluate the solutions and the plan, maintain the gains by standardizing the process, and outline steps for on-going improvements including opportunities for replication. The output is:

1. Before and after analysis

2. A monitoring system

3. Completed documentation of results, learnings, and recommendations.

Phase 1: DEFINE

In Phase 1: **Define**, you will be setting project goals and boundaries based on your knowledge of your organization's business goals, customer needs, and the process that needs to be improved to get you to a higher sigma level.

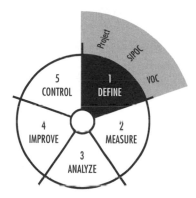

The tools most commonly used in the Define phase are:

1. Project charter (including the business case)
2. Stakeholder analysis
3. SIPOC
4. Rolled Throughput Yield
5. Voice of the Customer
6. Affinity Diagram
7. Kano Model
8. Critical-to-Quality (CTQ) tree

PROJECT CHARTER

The charter is a contract between the organization's leadership and the team created at the outset of the project. Its purpose is:

- To clarify what is expected of the team
- To keep the team focused
- To keep the team aligned with organizational priorities
- To transfer the project from the champion to the team

Elements of the Charter:
- Business case (financial impact)
- Problem statement
- Goal statement
- Project scope
- Roles of team members
- Milestones/deliverables
- Support required

BUSINESS CASE

Because of limited resources, teams should be assigned to projects with a significant financial impact. Rough estimates can be used. Examples of categories of financial impact follow.

POTENTIAL IMPROVEMENT	POTENTIAL IMPACT
Reduce inventory levels	Reduce capital investment in inventory
Reduce time-to-market	Increase revenues through increased sales
Reduce equipment downtime	Increase capacity
Reduce rejects/rework	Decrease material costs; greater ROI
Speed up delivery time	Increase revenues

Teams should be aware that these estimates are likely to change as the team finds out more about the problem, and the problem becomes more focused. It is strongly advised that these calculations be made with the assistance of the Finance Department.

STAKEHOLDER ANALYSIS

A DMAIC project will require a fundamental change in the process. In an effort to mitigate the resistance to change when the improvement is implemented, it is crucial to identify the stakeholders early on, and to develop a communication plan for each of them. Typical stakeholders include managers, people who work in the process under study, upstream and downstream departments, customers, suppliers and finance. Regular communication can create more buy-in, identify better solutions, and avoid pitfalls.

The team can create a commitment scale to identify the groups involved or affected by the change, identify the amount of work required to bring groups to the level of commitment needed for the successful implementation of the change, and to help set priorities and develop communication plans. An example follows.

Left side lists typical
levels of commitment

People or groups
listed across top

LEVEL OF COMMITMENT	PEOPLE OR GROUPS		
	SALES	MGMT.	CUST.
Enthusiastic support Will work hard to make it happen	●		◉
Help it work Will lend appropriate support to implement solution		●	
Compliant Will do minimal acceptable and will tend to erode the standard			●
Hesitant Holds some reservations; won't volunteer			
Indifferent Won't help; won't hurt			**X**
Uncooperative Will have to be prodded		**X**	
Opposed Will openly act on and state opposition to the solution	**X**		
Hostile Will block implementation of the solution at all costs			

The Dot shows level of commitment needed for
successful completion.

The X shows current level of commitment.

The Line emphasizes amount of change needed.

The team should note that not every group needs to be brought to the level of enthusiastic support for successful implementation.

SIPOC

A SIPOC is a high-level process map that includes **S**uppliers, **I**nputs, **P**rocess, **O**utputs, and **C**ustomers. Quality is judged based on the output of a process. The quality of the output is improved by analyzing input and process variables.

SIPOC is a very effective communications tool. It ensures that the team members are all viewing the process in the same way. It also informs leadership of exactly what the team is working on. Therefore, it should be done in the early stages of the project.

The process is bounded with this tool. The process is mapped at a high level (4–7 steps). Then working from the right, identify the customers, the output, the input and the suppliers. An example follows.

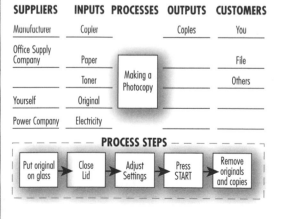

SUPPLIERS	INPUTS	PROCESSES	OUTPUTS	CUSTOMERS
Manufacturer	Copier		Copies	You
Office Supply Company	Paper	Making a Photocopy		File
	Toner			Others
Yourself	Original			
Power Company	Electricity			

PROCESS STEPS

Put original on glass → Close Lid → Adjust Settings → Press START → Remove originals and copies

Questions that might help with SIPOC:
- **Purpose** — Why does this process exist?
- **Outputs** — What product/service does this process make?
- **Customers** — Who uses the products from this process?
- **Inputs/Suppliers** — Where does the information or material you work on come from? Who are your suppliers? What do they supply?
- **Process steps** — What happens to each input?

How to construct a SIPOC
- Name the process
- Clarify the start and stop (boundaries) of the process
- List key outputs and customers
- List key inputs and suppliers
- Identify, name, and order the major process steps

ROLLED THROUGHPUT YIELD

Often in manufacturing, the calculation of rolled throughput yield can help to focus the problem. Here is an example.

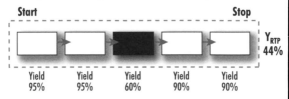

How to calculate rolled throughput yield
- Calculate yield for each process step
- Calculate **R**olled **T**hroughput **Y**ield (**RTY**) to establish a baseline for the entire process by multiplying the yield from each step

· Revisit your project scope
· Significant differences in yield suggest creating a new map for the subprocess with the lowest yield

VOICE OF THE CUSTOMER

Voice of the Customer (**VOC**) is used to describe customers' needs and their perceptions of your product or service. The VOC is critical to an organization to:

· Decide what products and services to offer
· Identify critical features and specifications for those products and services
· Decide where to focus improvement efforts
· Get a baseline in measure of customer satisfaction to measure improvement against
· Identify key drivers of customer satisfaction

The process for VOC is

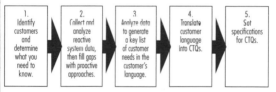

The outcomes are
· A list of customers and customer segments
· Identification of relevant reactive and proactive sources of data
· Verbal or numerical data that identify customer needs
· Defined Critical-to-Quality requirements (**CTQ**s)
· Specifications for each CTQ

THE VOC PLAN

List the main customers who use your product or service and make notes about potential segments that might be relevant to your project. Make sure you include all relevant internal and external customers (for example, intermediate customers such as logistics providers, warehousing, etc.).

Think about what you need to know from these customers.

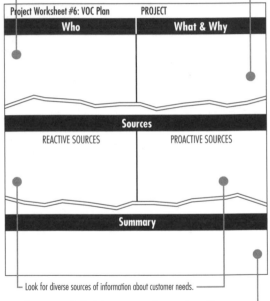

Project Worksheet #6: VOC Plan — PROJECT

Who	What & Why

Sources

REACTIVE SOURCES	PROACTIVE SOURCES

Summary

Look for diverse sources of information about customer needs.

Summarize specifically which customers you will contact, when, and how.

Reactive sources include such things as customer complaints, service calls, and warranty claims.

Proactive sources include such things as interviews, focus groups, and surveys.

It is helpful to summarize this information by using an **Affinity Diagram**.

AFFINITY DIAGRAM

An Affinity Diagram is a tool that organizes language data into related groups. It stresses creative or intuitive thinking. Here are its features:

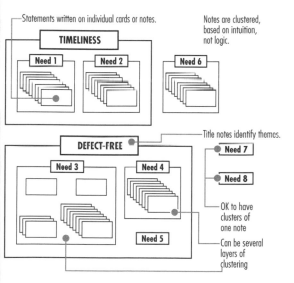

Statements written on individual cards or notes.

Notes are clustered, based on intuition, not logic.

TIMELINESS

Need 1   Need 2   Need 6

DEFECT-FREE

Need 3   Need 4

Need 5

Title notes identify themes.

Need 7

Need 8

OK to have clusters of one note

Can be several layers of clustering

Why create an affinity diagram:
· Encourages breakthrough thinking

- Helps to identify patterns in mountains of data
- Allows us to gather large amounts of language data
- Can be used to organize ideas, issues, and opinions
- Encourages ownership of results

When to use an affinity diagram:
- Analyzing qualitative customer data
- Dealing with complex problems or issues
- Organizing ideas, issues, and opinions

How to Construct an Affinity Diagram
- Statements are written on individual cards or notes.
- Notes are clustered based on intuition, not logic. Do this silently. If you disagree with a note's placement, move it. If you disagree with where someone moves a note, move it back.
- Clusters of notes are given titles, which identify themes. There can be several layers of clusters.
- One note can be a cluster if it is not related to any other notes.

An example:

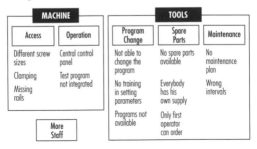

KANO MODEL

Noriaki Kano is a renowned Japanese expert in total quality management. His practical experience with understanding customer requirements led him to define three categories of customer needs:

- **Must Be** — These needs are expected by the customer. If they are unfulfilled, the customer will be dissatisfied, but even if they are completely fulfilled the customer would not be particularly satisfied (e.g., airline safety).
- **More Is Better** — These needs have a linear effect on customer satisfaction. The more these needs are met, the more satisfied these customers are (e.g., cheap airline tickets).
- **Delighters** — These needs do not cause dissatisfaction when not present but satisfy the customer when they are (e.g., airline that serves hot chocolate chip cookies en route).

This is what the Kano Model looks like:

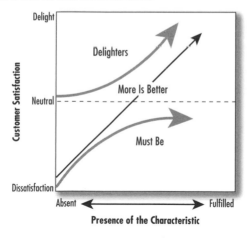

The Kano Model and VOC
- Must be characteristics are generally taken for granted, unless they are absent.
- Customers generally discuss or bring up issues related to More is Better characteristics.
- Delighters are generally not mentioned, since the customers are not dissatisfied with their absence.

CTQ TREE

A CTQ tree is a tool that aids in translating customer language into quantified requirements for our product/service. Here is an example:

Why create a CTQ Tree
- Translates broad customer requirements into specific critical-to-quality (CTQ) requirements
- Helps the team to move from high-level to detailed specifications
- Ensures that all aspects of the need are identified

When to use a CTQ Tree:
- Unspecific customer requirements
- Complex, broad needs

An example of the need for good customer service follows.

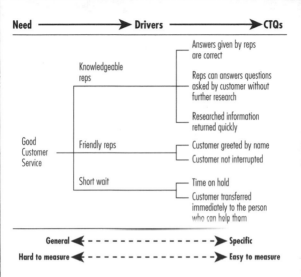

Need ————————➤	Drivers ————————➤	CTQs

Good Customer Service

Knowledgeable reps
- Answers given by reps are correct
- Reps can answers questions asked by customer without further research
- Researched information returned quickly

Friendly reps
- Customer greeted by name
- Customer not interrupted

Short wait
- Time on hold
- Customer transferred immediately to the person who can help them

General ◄ - - - - - - - - - - - - - ➤ Specific

Hard to measure ◄ - - - - - - - - - - - - - ➤ Easy to measure

Setting Specifications for CTQs

In manufacturing, specification limits often come from technical or mechanical requirements. Otherwise, base specification limits on data about customer needs set specifications where customer satisfaction starts to fall off appreciably.

Specifications can either be one-sided or two-sided. If there is a single value that the process output should not go above or below, it is a single-sided specification. If you can define both a lower and upper boundary, you have two-sided specifications.

By following the five-step VOC data collection process, we can help ensure that we have understood the current situation from the customer's perspective.

COMPLETION CHECKLIST

By the end of Phase 1: **Define**, you should be able to describe for your sponsor:

- Why this project is important
- What business goals the project must achieve to be considered successful
- Who the players are on the project (sponsors, advisors, team leader, team members)
- What limitations (budget, time, resources) have been placed on this project
- What key process is involved (including its Suppliers, Input, Outputs, and Customers)
- What the current process yield is
- What the customer requirements or specifications are

Phase 2: MEASURE

The **Define** phase has produced a team charter, an overview of the process to be improved, and information on what is critical to quality for customers. In Phase 2: **Measure**, the goal is to pinpoint the location or source of problems as precisely as you can by building a factual understanding of existing process conditions and problems. That knowledge will help you narrow the range of potential causes you need to investigate in the **Analyze** phase. An important part of the Measure phase is to establish a baseline capability level.

The tools used most commonly in the Measure phase are:

1. Data Collection Plan
2. Data Collection Forms
3. Control Charts
4. Frequency Plots
5. Gage R&R
6. Pareto Charts
7. Prioritization Matrix
8. FMEA

9. Process Capability
10. Process Sigma
11. Sampling
12. Stratification
13. Time Series Plots (Run Charts)

DATA COLLECTION

In planning for data collection it will be important to:
- Be able to identify possible measures
- Know how to select the most important variables to measure
- Know how to create a data collection plan
- Be able to identify stratification factors for a given problem
- Know the various types of data
- Be able to create and use operational definitions
- Be able to create a useful data collection form

Desired data characteristics are:
- Sufficient
- Relevant
- Representative
- Contextual

One of the most important things a team can do in planning for data collection is to draw and label the graph that will communicate the findings before the collection begins. This points you to exactly what data you need. Moreover, it raises questions that you might not have thought of, which you can add to your plan. This will prevent having to go back for data that you hadn't thought of.

Data Collection Plan   Project _____

What questions do you want to answer?

Being clear about your question will help you make sure you collect the right data.

Data		Operational Definition and Procedures			
What	Measure type/ Data type	How measured?	Related conditions to record*	Sampling notes	How/where recorded (attach form)

Recording what data you are going to collect reminds you what you want to accomplish. Noting the type of data helps you decide how you should analyze the data.

An operational definition defines exactly how you will go about collecting and recording the data.

*Related conditions are stratification variables.

How will you ensure consistency?	What is your plan for starting data collection? (Attach details if necessary.)
What will you do to make sure the data collected at one point in time is comparable to data collected at other times? That is, that no biases have been introduced in the way the data are collected?	Just how will you go about collecting the data? Thinking about how you will display the data will help you make sure you are getting the right kind of data to answer the question you have in mind.

IDENTIFY KEY MEASURES AND CLARIFY GOALS

Step 1 of data collection is to identify the key measures and clarify goals. The goal here is to make sure the data you collect will give you the answers you need. The "right" information: describes the problem you're studying; describes related conditions that might provide clues about causes; can be analyzed in ways that answer your questions.

In the equation $Y = f(X_1, X_2, X_3....X_n)$, Y relates to the process output. It tells us how well we are meeting customer needs.

X relates to the various input and process variables. We must gain this knowledge in order to improve the process. Understanding the variation in the output variable (Y) requires data about the Xs.

Since data collection can consume a tremendous amount of time, it is critical to focus on the key measures. The high-level SIPOC map provides a starting point for identifying possible measures. Other funneling tools might be necessary. The two funneling tools, Prioritization Matrix and FMEA follow.

PRIORITIZATION MATRIX

There are two applications for a prioritization matrix:

1. Linking output variables to customer requirements, and
2. Linking input and process variables to output variables

The second application is used for identifying key measures.

Why use a prioritization matrix

- To identify the critical few variables that need to be measured and analyzed
- To help to focus the data collection effort
- To help formulate theories about causes and effects

©2002 Rath & Strong/Aon Management Consulting

When to use a prioritization matrix
- There are too many variables that might have an impact on the output of the process.
- Collecting data about all possible variables would cost too much time and money.
- Team members have different theories about what happens in the process.

How to construct a prioritization matrix
1. List all output variables.
2. Rank and weight the output variables.
3. List all input and process variables.
4. Evaluate the strength of the relationship between output and input/process variable (correlation factor).
5. Cross-multiply weight and correlation factor.
6. Highlight the critical few variables.

THE PRIORITIZATION MATRIX

Output Variables							Total
Weight							

(left axis label: Process / Input Variables)

FMEA

Failure **M**ode and **E**ffect **A**nalysis (FMEA) is another funneling tool. While it is most commonly used in designing a new product or service, it can be an effective tool for focusing the data collection effort on those input and process variables that are critical for the current process. Thus, it can be used in the Measure phase as well as the Improve phase. It is a structured approach to identify, estimate, prioritize and evaluate risk. It aims at failure prevention.

Why use an FMEA
- Identifies the critical input and process variables that can affect output quality

- Establishes priorities and guides the data collection effort
- Evaluates the risk associated with defects
- Helps to formulate assumptions about the relationship between variables

When to use FMEA
- Lack of clarity about what the important variables are and how they affect output quality
- Need to prioritize data collection effort

How to construct a FMEA
1. Identify potential failure modes — ways in which the product, service, or process might fail.
2. Identify potential effect of each failure (consequences of that failure) and rate its severity
3. Identify causes of the effects and rate their likelihood of occurrence.
4. Rate your ability to detect each failure mode.
5. Multiply the three numbers together to determine the risk of each failure mode (**RPN** = **R**isk **P**riority **N**umber).
6. Identify ways to reduce or eliminate risk associated with high RPNs.

Sample Severity Rating Scale
(Severity = likely impact of the failure)

	Rating	Criteria: A failure could...
Bad	10	Injure a customer or employee
	9	Be illegal
	8	Render the product or service unfit for use
	7	Cause extreme customer dissatisfaction
	6	Result in partial malfunction
	5	Cause a loss of performance likely to result in a complaint
	4	Cause minor performance loss
	3	Cause a minor nuisance; can be overcome with no loss
	2	Be unnoticed; minor effect on performance
Good	1	Be unnoticed and not affect the performance

©2002 Rath & Strong/Aon Management Consulting

Sample Occurrence Rating Scale

	Rating	Time Period	Probability
Bad	10	More than once per day	> 30%
	9	Once every 3-4 days	≤ 30%
	8	Once per week	≤ 5%
	7	Once per month	≤ 1%
	6	Once every 3 months	≤ .03%
	5	Once every 6 months	≤ 1 per 10,000
	4	Once per year	< 6 per 100,000
	3	Once every 1-3 years	≤ 6 per million
	2	Once every 3-6 years	≤ 3 per 10 million
Good	1	Once every 6-100 years	≤ 2 per billion

Sample Detection Rating Scale

Rating	Criteria: A failure could...
Bad 10	Defect caused by failure is not detectable
9	Occasional units are checked for defects
8	Units are systematically sampled and inspected
7	All units are manually inspected
6	Manual inspection with mistake-proofing modifications
5	Process is monitored (SPC) and manually inspected
4	SPC used with an immediate reaction to out of control conditions
3	SPC as above with 100% inspection surrounding out of control conditions
2	All units are automatically inspected
Good 1	Defect is obvious and can be kept from affecting customer

THE FMEA FORM

FMEA Analysis

Project: _____
Team: _____

Date: _____ (original)
_____ (revised)

Item or Process Step	Potential Failure Mode	Potential Effects of Failure	Severity	Potential Causes	Occurrence	Current Controls	Detection	RPN	Recommended Action	Responsibility and Target Date	"After" Action Taken	Severity	Occurrence	Detection	RPN

Total Risk Priority Number: _____

"After" Risk Priority Number: _____

STRATIFICATION

Stratification means dividing data into groups (strata) based on key characteristics. A "key characteristic" is some aspect of the data that you think could help explain when, where, and why a problem exists. The purpose of dividing data into groups is to detect a pattern that localizes a problem or explains why the frequency of impact varies between times, locations, or conditions.

Ways to stratify data:
The typical groups are based on:

- **Who** — which people, groups of people, departments, or organization are involved

- **What** — machines, equipment, products, services, supplies

- **Where** — physical location of the defect

- **When** — time of day, day of the week, step of the process

In the Analyze phase we will address how to analyze stratified data. Here we will preview a display of stratified data. The example on the next page shows the elapsed time to complete lubes in all locations, then stratified by location A, B, and C. It shows that location B takes less time and has less variation that the other two locations.

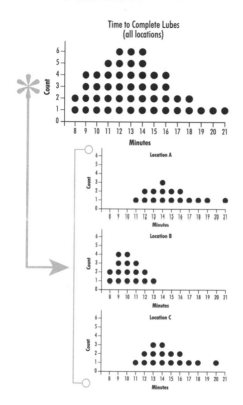

Time to Complete Lubes
(all locations)

TYPES OF DATA

Continuous Data

Often obtained by use of a measuring system

The usefulness of the data depends on the quality of the measurement system

Counts of non-occurrences are best treated as continuous data

Discrete Data

Includes percentages, counts, attribute, and ordinal

Percentages = the proportion of items with a given characteristic; need to be able to count both occurrences and non-occurrences

For count data, it is impossible or impractical to count a non-occurrence; the event must be rare

Occurrences must be independent

Type/How Obtained	Examples		
Continuous: (or "variable") Measuring instrument or a calculation	**Service:**	Elapsed time to complete transaction, average length of phone calls
	Manufacturing:	Elapsed cycle time, metal purity, gauge production rates, weight, length, speed
	Both:	Budget vs. actual (dollars), average customer satisfaction score; amount purchased
Discrete: Percentage or proportion Count occurrences and non-occurrences	**Service:**	Proportion of late applications, incorrect invoices
	Manufacturing:	Proportion of defective items, reworked items, damaged items, late shipments
	Both:	Proportion of employees absent, incomplete orders
Discrete: Count Count occurrences in an area of opportunity	**Service:**	Number of applications, errors, complaints, etc.
	Manufacturing:	Number of computer malfunctions, machine breakdowns, accidents
Discrete: Attribute Observation	**Service:**	Type of application, type of request
	Manufacturing:	Type of product
	Both:	Type of customer, type of method used (new vs. old), location of activity
Discrete: Ordinal Observation or Ranking	**Both:**	Customer rating (1 = very satisfied/5 = very dissatisfied); day of week (MTWTF) date, time order

OPERATIONAL DEFINITIONS

Step 2 of Data Collection is to develop operational definitions and procedures. The goal is to make sure all the data collectors measure a characteristic in the same way. This removes ambiguity and reduces variation in the measurements.

An operational definition is a precise description that tells how to get a value for the characteristic you are trying to measure. It includes what something is and how to measure it.

The features of an operational definition are:
- Must be specific and concrete
- Must be measurable
- Must be useful to both you and your customer
- There is no single right answer.

The more specific the definition is, the better. Plan on refining the definition after you try it out. If you collect the data manually, training will help data collectors consistently apply operational definitions.

DATA COLLECTION FORMS

Checksheets are basic forms that help standardize data collection by providing specific spaces where people should record data.

Defines what data is being collected ———→ **Machine Downtime (Line 13)**

Operator: _____Wendy_____   Date: _____May 19_____

Reason	Frequency	Comments
Carton Transport	ⵌ ⵌ II	
Metal Check	IIII	
No Product	ⵌ I	←
Sealing Unit	II	
Barcoding	III	
Conveyor Belt		
Bad Product	ⵌ	Burned flakes III Low weight II
Other	II	

Lists the characteristics or conditions of interest

Includes place to put the data

May want to add space for tracking stratification factors

Has room for comments

FREQUENCY PLOT CHECKSHEET

A frequency plot checksheet is a special type of checksheet used for numerical data. It creates a picture that shows how often different data values appear.

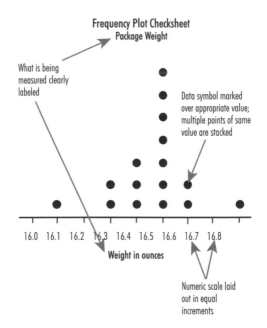

Frequency Plot Checksheet
Package Weight

What is being measured clearly labeled

Data symbol marked over appropriate value; multiple points of same value are stacked

Weight in ounces

Numeric scale laid out in equal increments

16.0 16.1 16.2 16.3 16.4 16.5 16.6 16.7 16.8

CONFIRMATION CHECKSHEET

A confirmation checksheet is a special type of checksheet used to confirm that steps in a process have been completed and to collect data on time taken in different process steps.

Lists process steps **Report Preparation Confirmation Checksheet**

Step	Done?	Completion Data				Notes
		Planned date	Actual date	Planned duration	Actual duration	
Project completed	✓	6-12	6-26	N/A	N/A	Cust requested changes
Client review and approval	✓	6-17	7-6	5d	10d	Client personnel on vacation
Final report, draft	✓	6-30	7-21	13d	15d	
Final report, review	✓	7-12	7-20	12d	7d	
Final report revisions	✓	7-21	8-2	9d	5d	Minor changes requested
Desktop publishing of report		7-28		7d		
Final report		7-30		2d		

Shows where you are in the process

Captures data on time taken to complete steps; lets you track differences between planned and actuals

Notes may help explain differences between planned and actuals

CONCENTRATION DIAGRAM

A concentration diagram is a data collection form where you write directly on a picture of an object, form, or work area.

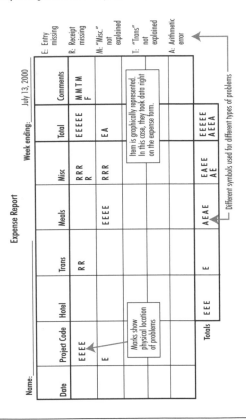

Expense Report

Name: _____   Week ending: _____ July 13, 2000

Date	Project Code	Hotel	Trans	Meals	Misc	Total	Comments
	E E E E		R R		R R R R	E E E E E	M M T M F
	E			E E E E	R R R	E A	
Totals		E E E	E	A E A E	E A E E A E	E E E E E A E A A	

Marks show physical location of problems

Item is graphically represented. In this case, they took data right on the expense form.

Different symbols used for different types of problems

E: Entry missing
R: Receipt missing
M: "Misc." not explained
T: "Trans" not explained
A: Arithmetic error

VALIDATING THE MEASUREMENT SYSTEM: GAGE R&R

Step 3 of Data Collection is to validate the measurement system. The goal is to minimize controllable factors that could exaggerate the amount of variation in data.

Measurements should be...	Typical Problem
Precise/Accurate The measurement method or device does not vary much from the actual value	**Inaccurate** The measurement method or device results in values that vary greatly from the actual value
Repeatable Repeated measurements on the same item or characteristic by the same person lead to the same result	**Unrepeatable** Repeated measurements on the same item or characteristic lead to different results
Reproducible Two or more people measuring the same characteristic in the same way get the same result	**Unreproducible** Two or more people measuring the same characteristic in the same way get different results
Stable Over Time The measurement system does not change over time	**Unstable Over Time** The measurement system does varies over time

A Gage R&R Study is a set of trials conducted to assess the Repeatability and Reproducibility of your measurement system.

- Multiple operators measure multiple units a multiple number of times
- Example: 3 operators each measure 7 units twice
- "Blindness" is extremely desirable. It is better that the operator not know that the part being measured is part of a special test. At a minimum they should not know which of the test parts they are currently measuring.

You analyze the variation in the study results to determine how much of it comes from differences in the operators, techniques, or the units themselves.

Common Problems with measurement systems

- **Bias or inaccuracy** —The measurements have a different average value than a "standard" method.
- **Imprecision** — Repeated readings on the same material vary too much in relation to current process variation.
- **Not reproducible** — The measurement process is different for different operators, or measuring devices or labs. This may be either a difference in bias or precision.
- **Unstable measurement system over time** — Either the bias or the precision changes over time.
- **Lack of resolution** — The measurement process cannot measure to precise enough units to capture current product variation.

Desired characteristics for continuous variables

Accuracy —The measured value has little deviation from the actual value. Accuracy is usually tested by comparing an average of repeated measurements to a known standard value for that unit.

Repeatability — The same person taking a measurement on the same unit gets the same result.

Reproducibility — Other people (or other instruments or labs) get the same result you get when measuring the same item or characteristic.

Stability — Measurements taken by a single person in the same way vary little over time.

Adequate Resolution — There is enough resolution in the measurement device so that the product can have many different values.

A measurement system consists of:
- Measuring devices
- Procedures
- Definitions
- People

To improve a measurement system, you need to:
- Evaluate how well it works now (by asking "how much of the variation we see in our data is due to measurement system?").
- Evaluate the results and develop improvement strategies.

WAYS TO SEE IF THE MEASUREMENT SYSTEM IS ADEQUATE

Test for...	How
1. Accuracy	Test for the amount of bias throughout the product range by repeatedly measuring "known" quantities.
2. Repeatability	Have the same sample measured repeatedly by the same person. This reveals the variation in the measurement device.
3. Reproducibility	Have many people (instruments or labs) measure the same sample repeatedly.
4. Stability	Have the same person measure the same item over time. Look for special causes that would indicate lack of stability.
5. Adequate Resolution	Make sure 5 or more distinct values are observed within the range of product variation in any of the above tests.

Data for a Gage R&R Study
- Each operator measures each unit repeatedly.
- Data must be balanced — each operator must measure each unit the same number of times.
- The units should represent the range of variation in the process.
- Operators should randomly and "blindly" test the units; they should not know which unit they are measuring when they record their results.

ASSESSING THE ACCURACY, REPEATABILITY, AND REPRODUCIBILITY OF A DISCRETE MEASUREMENT SYSTEM

- Discrete data are usually the result of human judgment ("which category does this item belong in?").
- When categorizing items (good/bad; type of call; reason for leaving), you need a high degree of agreement on which way an item should be categorized.
- The best way to assess human judgment is to have all operators categorize several known test units.
  - Look for 100% agreement.
  - Use disagreements as opportunities to determine and eliminate problems.

BEGIN DATA COLLECTION

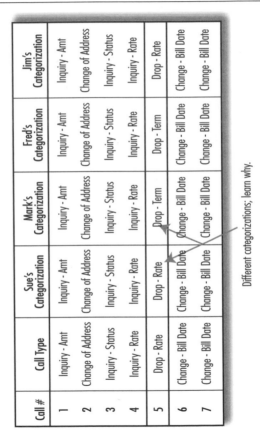

Call #	Call Type	Sue's Categorization	Mark's Categorization	Fred's Categorization	Jim's Categorization
1	Inquiry - Amt	Inquiry - Amt	Inquiry - Amt	Inquiry - Amt	Inquiry - Amt
2	Change of Address	Change of Address	Change of Address	Change of Address	Change of Address
3	Inquiry - Status	Inquiry - Status	Inquiry - Status	Inquiry - Status	Inquiry - Status
4	Inquiry - Rate	Inquiry - Rate	Inquiry - Rate	Inquiry - Rate	Inquiry - Rate
5	Drop - Rate	Drop - Rate	Drop - Term	Drop - Term	Drop - Rate
6	Change - Bill Date	Change - Bill Date	Change - Bill Date	Change - Bill Date	Change - Bill Date
7	Change - Bill Date	Change - Bill Date	Change - Bill Date	Change - Bill Date	Change - Bill Date

Different categorizations; learn why.

Step 4 of data collection is to actually begin the collection. The goal is to ensure a smooth start-up. It requires that you:
- Train the data collectors.
- Error-proof data collection procedures. It helps to pilot and test the data collection forms and procedures.
- Be there in the beginning.
- Decide how you will display your data.

Continue Improving Measurement Consistency
Step 5 of data collection is to continue improving measurement consistency. The goal is to check that data collection procedures are being followed and that changes are made as necessary to adapt to changing conditions. Questions you should ask are:
- Are measurements consistent? How do you know?
- Repeatable
- Reproducible
- Stable
- Do the data exhibit strange features?

DEVELOPING A SAMPLING STRATEGY

Sampling is collecting a portion of all the data using that portion to draw conclusions. Sound conclusions can often be drawn from a relatively small amount of data. We sample because looking at all the data may be too expensive, too time-consuming, or destructive (e.g., taste tests). Sampling is used in every phase of DMAIC where data are collected.

The first question asked is "How many samples do I need?" The answer depends on four factors:

- Type of data — discrete or continuous
- What you want to do
  - Describe a characteristic for a whole group (mean or proportion). Within a certain precision (+/– ___ units).
  - Compare group characteristics (find difference between group means or proportions; at what power — the probability you want of detecting a certain difference).
- What you guess the standard deviation (or proportion) will be
- How confident you want to be (usually 95%)

There is a trade-off between precision, sample size, and cost.

The formulas for sample size were developed for population sampling. They can be applied to process sampling if the process is stable. Since most processes are not stable, the results of the formulas should be used as the lowest figure you should consider.

Purpose of Sample	Formula / Minitab Commands
Estimate average (e.g., determine baseline cycle time)	$n = \left(\dfrac{2s}{d} \right)^2$ (Where d = precision ± ___ units)
Estimate proportion (e.g., determine baseline % defective)	$n = \left(\dfrac{2}{d} \right)^2 (p)(1-p)$ (Where d = precision ± ___ units)

The formulas are as follows:

d = precision   p = proportion

n = sample size   s = standard deviation

For conclusions to be valid, samples must be representative.
- Data should fairly represent the process.
- No systematic differences should exist between the data you collect and the data you don't collect.

A representative sample requires planning. Consider:
- What groups to sample, and the proportion of each group in the sample
- When to sample and/or how often to sample
- Where to sample

In DMAIC we are usually sampling from a process. We want to ensure that we can see the behavior of the process. So we:
- Sample systematically or with subgroups (not randomly) across time. Systematic or subgroup sampling ensures the sample will be representative of the process because each time period is represented.
- Try to sample from enough time periods to fairly represent the sources of variation in the process.
- Generally, collect small samples more frequently to ensure that the process behavior is represented fairly over time.
- Make a control chart or time plot to determine if the process is stable or unstable (look for outliers, shifts, trends, or other patterns).

SAMPLING APPROACHES

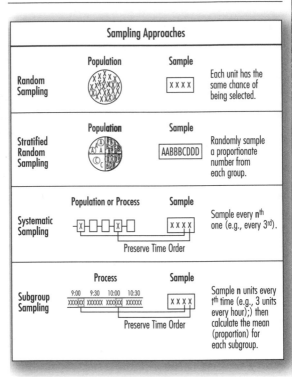

Sampling Approaches			
Random Sampling	Population	Sample	Each unit has the same chance of being selected.
Stratified Random Sampling	Population	Sample	Randomly sample a proportionate number from each group.
Systematic Sampling	Population or Process	Sample	Sample every **n**th one (e.g., every 3rd).
Subgroup Sampling	Process	Sample	Sample **n** units every t^th time (e.g., 3 units every hour;) then calculate the mean (proportion) for each subgroup.

SUMMARY OF SAMPLING SITUATIONS

	Population	Process
Purpose	Estimate characteristic (average or proportion) Make comparisons (hypothesis testing)	Take action to make improvements Predict the future behavior of the process
Approach	Random sampling Stratified random sampling Systematic sampling	Systematic sampling Subgroup sampling

Considerations	Representativeness
	Discrete or continuous
	Estimate of **s** or **p**
	Desired prevision (**d**) or desired power
	Groups
	Cost
		Preserve time order to fairly represent process behavior
		Process stable or not
		Low- or high-volume process
		Rational basis for subgroup
		   Time-related sources of variation, or typical cycles
		   Subgroup size
		Sample groups from some time period
		Cost

Sample Size	To estimate average $$n = \left(\frac{2s}{d}\right)^2$$ To estimate proportions $$n = \left(\frac{2}{d}\right)^2 (p)(1-p)$$	If process is stable, use formulas for population sampling (left) If unstable take more data and plot it in time order

Very often the initial data you collect during an improvement project will be continuous data that have a natural time order. The first step in analyzing time-ordered data is to create a time plot or control chart. The next step is to create a frequency plot (also called a histogram) of the data and analyze the distribution.

If your data are not time-ordered, chances are you can use either a frequency plot or Pareto chart to analyze it.

- **Frequency plots** show the distribution of continuous numeric data.
- **Pareto charts** show the relative frequency or impact of data that can be divided into categories.

The goals of analyzing patterns in data are:

- Understand the relationship between quality and variation
- Be able to differentiate between common and special cause variation
- Be able to create and interpret time plots, control charts, histograms and Pareto Charts
- Understand the difference between control limits (process capability) and specification limits (customer requirements)

UNDERSTANDING VARIATION

When analyzing time-ordered data, you need to look at the variation, how the data values change from point to point. Certain patterns in the variation can provide clues about the source of process problems.

What is variation?

- No two anythings are exactly alike.
  - How a process is done will vary from day to day.
  - Measurements or counts collected on process output will vary over time.

- Quantifying the amount of variation in a process is a critical step towards improvement.
- Understanding what causes that variation helps us decide what kinds of actions are most likely to lead to lasting improvement.

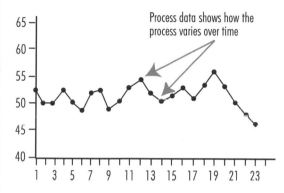

Process data shows how the process varies over time

The amount of variation in a process tells us what that process is actually capable of achieving. Specifications tell us what we want a process to be able to achieve. Traditionally, any value between the specifications was seen as good. The new view is that any time a characteristic deviates from the target, there is some loss. The bigger the deviation, the bigger the loss.

Special cause variation means something different happened at a certain time or place. **Common cause** variation is always present to some degree in the process. The goal is to minimize the variation. It is important to distinguish between special and common cause variation, because each requires a different strategy.

Special cause strategy is:
- Get timely data.
- Take immediate action to remedy any damage.
- Immediately search for a cause. Find out what was different on that occasion. Isolate the deepest cause you can affect.
- Develop a longer-term remedy that will prevent that special cause from recurring. Or, if results are good, retain that lesson.

Common cause strategy is improving a stable process. The process below is stable, but it does not meet customer needs.

Improving a stable process
Common causes of variation can hardly ever be reduced by attempts to explain the difference between individual points if the process is in statistical control. All the data are relevant. A process in statistical control usually requires fundamental changes for improvement. Using the DMAIC method can help you make fundamental changes in the process.

Effective improvement relies on being able to distinguish common cause variation from special cause variation.

- If you treat special causes like common causes, you lose an opportunity to track down and eliminate something specific that is increasing variation in your process.

- If you treat common causes like special causes, you will most likely end up increasing variation.

- Taking the wrong action not only doesn't improve the situation, it usually makes it worse.

COMMON AND SPECIAL CAUSE VARIATION

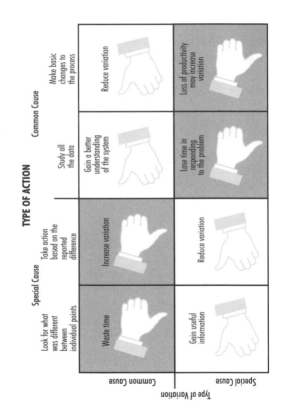

TYPE OF ACTION

	Special Cause		Common Cause	
	Look for what was different between individual points	Take action based on the reported difference	Study all the data	Make basic changes to the process
Common Cause	Waste time	Increase variation	Gain a better understanding of the system	Reduce variation
Special cause	Gain useful information	Reduce variation	Lose time in responding to the problem	Loss of productivity may increase variation

Type of Variation

TIME SERIES PLOTS (RUN CHARTS)

Why use a run chart
- To study observed data for trends or patterns over a specified period of time
- To focus attention on truly vital changes in the process
- To track useful information for predicting trends

When to use a run chart
- To understand variation of the process
- To compare a performance measure before and after implementation of a solution to measure the impact
- To detect trends, shifts, and cycles in the process

How to construct a run chart
1. Decide on the measure you want to analyze.
2. Gather data (minimum 20 data points).
3. Create a graph with a vertical line and a horizontal line.
4. On the vertical line (y-axis), draw the scale related to the variable you are measuring.
5. On the horizontal line (x-axis), draw the time or sequence scale.
6. Calculate the median and draw a horizontal line at the median value.
7. Plot the data in time order or sequence.
8. Identify runs (ignoring points on the median).
9. Check the table for run charts.

TIME PLOT FEATURES

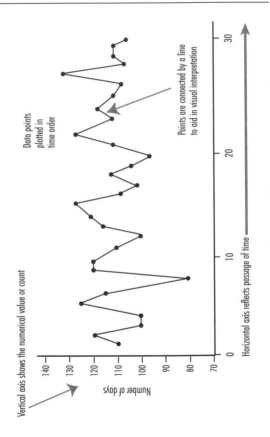

Vertical axis shows the numerical value or count

Data points plotted in time order

Points are connected by a line to aid in visual interpretation

Number of days

Horizontal axis reflects passage of time

COUNTING RUNS ON A TIME PLOT

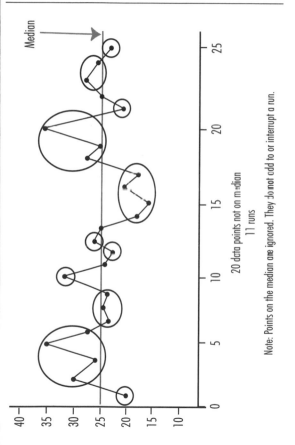

Median

20 data points not on median
11 runs

Note: Points on the median are ignored. They do not add to or interrupt a run.

A "run" is a series of points on the same side of the median.
- A run can be any length from 1 point to many points.

Too few or too many runs are important signals of special causes — they indicate something in the process has changed.

Because you often count runs on a time plot, they are also called run charts. In this example, there are 5 data points on the median, which are ignored because they neither add to nor interrupt any runs. That leaves 20 data points that are counted for the runs test, and 11 runs in the example shown here.

The number of runs you expect to see in a stable process depends on the number of data points. This chart shows how many runs could be expected when only common cause variation is present.

In the chart from the previous page for instance, there were 20 data points not on the median and 11 runs. That is well within the range of 6 – 14 listed in this table, so we can reasonably conclude there are no special causes of variation based on this test.

RUNS ABOVE AND BELOW THE MEDIAN

Number of data points not on median	Lower limit for number of runs	Upper limit for number of runs	Number of data points not on median	Lower limit for number of runs	Upper limit for number of runs
10	3	8	35	12	23
11	3	9	35	13	23
12	3	10	36	13	24
13	4	10	37	13	25
14	4	11	38	14	25
15	4	12	39	14	26
16	5	12	40	15	26
17	5	13	41	16	26
18	6	13	42	16	27
19	6	14	43	17	77
20	6	14	44	17	28
21	7	15	45	17	29
22	7	16	46	17	30
23	8	16	47	18	30
24	8	17	48	18	31
25	9	17	49	19	31
26	9	18	50	19	32
27	9	19	60	24	37
28	10	19	70	28	43
29	10	20	80	33	48
30	11	20	90	37	54
31	11	21	100	42	59
32	11	22	110	46	65
33	11	22	120	51	70

Signals of special cause on time plots:

- Too many or too few runs
- 6 or more points in a row continuously increasing or decreasing ("trend")

- 8 or more points in a row on the same side of the median ("shift")
- 14 or more points in a row alternating up and down

CONTROL CHART (INDIVIDUALS)

A **control chart** plots time-ordered data (just like run charts). Statistically determined control limits are drawn on the plot. The centerline calculation uses the mean not the median.

Why use a control chart
- Statistical control limits establish process capability.
- Statistical control limits are another way to separate common cause and special cause variation.
  - Points outside statistical limits signal a special cause.
- Can be used for almost any type of data collected over time
- Provides a common language for discussing process performance

When to use a control chart:
- Track performance over time
- Evaluate progress after process changes/improvements
- Focus attention on detecting and monitoring process variation over time

CONTROL CHART FEATURES

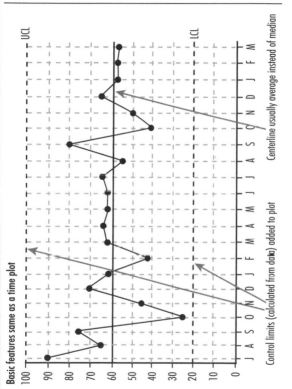

UCL

LCL

Centerline usually average instead of median

Control limits (calculated from data) added to plot

Basic features same as a time plot

J A S O N D J F M A M J J A S O N D J F M

HOW TO CONSTRUCT CONTROL CHARTS

- Select the process to be charted.
- Determine sampling method and plan.
- Initiate the data collection.
- Calculate the appropriate statistics.
- Plot the data values on the first chart (mean, median or individuals.
- Plot the range or standard deviation of the data on the second chart (only for continuous data).
- Interpret the control chart and determine if the process is "in control."

What are control limits?

- A **control limit** defines the bounds of common cause variation in the process.
- A control limit is a tool we use to help us take the right actions:
  - If all points are between the limits, we assume only common cause variation is present (unless one of the other signals of a Special Cause is present).
  - If a point falls outside the limit, you treat it as a special cause.
  - Otherwise, you do not investigate individual data points, but instead study the common cause variation in all data points.
- Control limits for individuals charts are calculated by the average +/–2.66 times the average of the moving range.

Control Charts and tests for special causes

- On a control chart, any data point outside the control limits is a signal of Special Cause.

- But can you use the previous Tests for special causes on a control chart too? The answer is, it depends.

- Two of the previous tests — counting "runs" and "8 points" — are determined relative to the **median** of the data. But on a control chart, the centerline is the **average**, not the median.

- Solution?

  – You can use the average with caution if you think the data have a roughly "Normal" distribution. "With caution" means to check your interpretation in other ways before taking action.

CONTROL CHARTS (X-BAR, R)

When data are collected in rational subgroups, it makes sense to use an **X-bar, R chart**. In the rational subgroup, we hope to have represented all the common causes of variation and none of the special causes of variation. X-bar, R charts allow us to detect smaller shifts than individuals charts. Also they allow us to clearly separate changes in process average from changes in process variability.

KEY PROPERTIES OF SUBGROUP DATA

Subgroup Data

		1	2	3	4	5	6	7	22	
Data	1	12.80	13.50	12.40	12.60	11.00	9.40	10.80	10.40	
	2	13.80	11.40	11.40	10.60	9.60	11.10	12.80	9.40	
	3	11.80	13.20	11.45	10.40	11.80	11.60	10.90	10.20	
	4	12.80	12.70	11.75	11.20	10.80	10.70	11.50	10.00	
	sum	51.20	50.80	47.00	44.80	43.20	42.80	46.00	40.00	
	$\overline{X}$	12.80	12.70	11.75	11.20	10.80	10.70	11.50	10.00	11.20
	R	2.00	2.10	1.00	2.20	2.20	2.20	2.00	1.00	

Average of the subgroup is noted as $\overline{X}$

Range within the subgroup, R

Average of the subgroup averages is noted as X-double-bar, $\overline{\overline{X}}$

An X-bar, R chart uses the variation within subgroups to establish limits for the averages of the subgroups.

When there is more variation between subgroups than within subgroups, a special cause will be signaled.

The X-bar chart will not detect special causes within a subgroup. Selection of the subgroups is of primary importance.

X-BAR, R CHART FEATURES

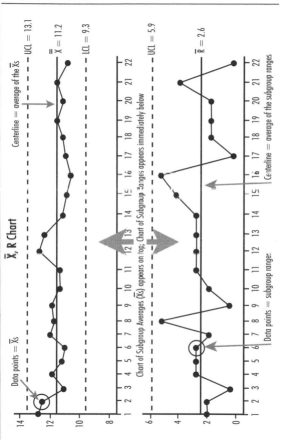

$\overline{X}$, R Chart

Centerline = average of the $\overline{X}$s

$\overline{\overline{X}} = 11.2$

UCL = 13.1

LCL = 9.3

Data points = $\overline{X}$s

Chart of Subgroup Averages ($\overline{X}$s) appears on top; Chart of Subgroup ranges appears immediately below

Centerline = average of the subgroup ranges

$\overline{R} = 2.6$

UCL = 5.9

Data points = subgroup ranges

CALCULATIONS FOR X-BAR, R CHARTS

| Number of Observations in Subgroup (n) | Factors for $\overline{X}$ Charts | | Factors for R Charts | |
| | $\hat{\sigma} = \overline{R}/d_2$ | Control Limits: $\overline{\overline{X}} = \pm A_2\overline{R}$ | Lower Control Limit: $D_3\overline{R}$ | Upper Control Limit: $D_4\overline{R}$ |
	d_2	A_2	D_3	D_4
2	1.128	1.880	0	3.267
3	1.693	1.023	0	2.575
4	2.059	0.729	0	2.282
5	2.326	0.577	0	2.115
6	2.534	0.483	0	2.004
7	2.704	0.419	0.076	1.924
8	2.847	0.373	0.136	1.864
9	2.970	0.337	0.184	1.816
10	3.078	0.308	0.223	1.777

Averages will always show less variability than individual values, so you expect the control limits on an X-bar chart to be narrower than limits for individual values. The constants noted above as d_2 and A_2 are the result of having less variability.

This above calculation table shows the formulas and constants used to calculate control limits for X-bar, R charts. As you can see, the lower control limit for the Range chart is always 0 until you have 7 or more data points in the subgroup.

Interpreting an X-bar, R chart
- Use the Signals of Special Causes on both charts.
- Look at the R chart first.
  - If the range chart is unstable (has special causes), the limits on the chart will be of little value.
  - If the range chart is unstable, it is unsafe to draw conclusions about variation in the process average.
- Look for positive or negative correlations between the data points on the X-bar and the R chart (both move in the same direction or in opposite directions for every point). This happens when the data have a skewed distribution, and some conclusions may be affected.

When to use X-bar, R charts
- Though used in both administrative and manufacturing applications, it is the tool of first choice in many manufacturing applications.
- Advantages over other charts:
  - Subgroups allow for a precise estimate of "local" variability.
  - Changes in process variability can be distinguished from changes in process average.
  - Small shifts in process average can be detected.

FREQUENCY PLOTS

A **frequency plot** shows the shape or distribution of the data by showing how often different values occur.

Why use frequency plots
- Summarizes data from a process and graphically presents the frequency distribution in bar form
- Helps to answer the question whether the process is capable of meeting customer requirements

When to use frequency plots
- To display large amounts of data that are difficult to interpret in tabular form
- To show the relative frequency of occurrence of the various data values
- To reveal the centering, spread and variation of the data
- To illustrate quickly the underlying distribution of the data

FREQUENCY PLOT FEATURES

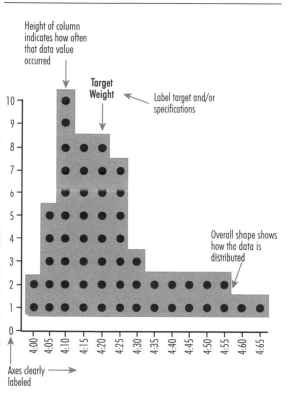

Height of column indicates how often that data value occurred

Target Weight

Label target and/or specifications

Overall shape shows how the data is distributed

Axes clearly labeled

TYPES OF FREQUENCY PLOTS:

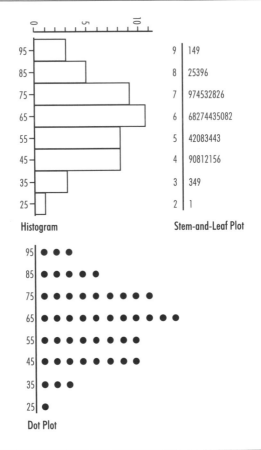

9	149	
8	25396	
7	974532826	
6	68274435082	
5	42083443	
4	90812156	
3	349	
2	1	

Histogram   Stem-and-Leaf Plot

Dot Plot

- Frequency plots come in a number of shapes and formats. The plots above show the same data displayed on three different types of frequency plots.

  – Plots where the height of a bar is used to denote the counts are commonly called **histograms**.

  – Plots where individual data values are indicated by simple symbols (X, tick mark, or l) are called **dot plots** (or simply "frequency plots").

  – **Stem-and-leaf plots** show the actual numeric values: major units to the left of the line (the "stem") and minor units to the right (the "leaves"). You can always tell the exact data values (e.g., 91, 94, 99, 82, 85, 83…).

- Construction methods for the different plots are quite similar.

- In the dot plot shown above, the tick mark labels (95, 85, 75…) indicate that the data values are clustered into units of 10. Anything between 20 and 29 is plotted at value 25, values between 30 and 39 are plotted at 35, etc.

  –This practice of clustering data values is common with frequency plots because the overall shape and distribution is usually more important to our understanding than the exact values.

How to construct a frequency plot

1. Decide on the process measure.

2. Gather data (at least 50 data points).

3. Prepare a frequency table of the data.

   a. Count the number of data points.

   b. Calculate the range.

   c. Determine the number of class intervals.

   d. Determine the class width.

   e. Construct the frequency table.

---

4. Draw a frequency plot (histogram) of the table.
5. Interpret the graph.

What to look for on a frequency plot
- Center of the data
- Range of the data
- Shape of the distribution
- Comparison with target and specifications
- Any irregularities

COMMON SHAPES OF FREQUENCY PLOTS: 1

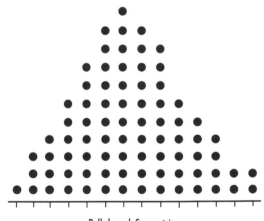

Bell shaped. Symmetric.

If a frequency plot shows a bell-shaped, symmetric distribution:

- **Conclude** — No special causes indicated by the distribution; data may come from a stable process (Caution: special causes may appear on a time plot or control chart).

- **Action** — Make fundamental changes to improve a stable process (common cause strategy).

COMMON SHAPES OF FREQUENCY PLOTS: 2

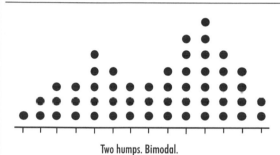

Two humps. Bimodal.

If a frequency plot shows a two-humped, bimodal distribution:

- **Conclude** — What we thought was one process operates like two processes (two sets of operating conditions with two sets of output).

- **Action** — Use stratification or other analysis techniques to seek out causes for two humps; be wary of reacting to a time plot or control chart for data with this distribution.

COMMON SHAPES OF FREQUENCY PLOTS: 3

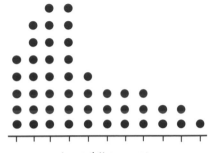

Long tail. Not symmetric.

If a frequency plot shows a long-tailed distribution (is not symmetric):

- **Conclude** — Data may come from a process that is not easily explained with simple mathematical assumptions (like normality). A long-tailed pattern is very common when measuring time or counting problems.

- **Action** — You'll need to use most data analysis techniques with caution when data has a long-tailed distribution. Some will lead to false conclusions.

- For example, the control limit calculations are based on the assumption that the data have a bell-shaped curved. Calculating control limits for data with a long-tailed distribution will likely make you overreact to common cause variation and miss some special causes. Other tests that rely on normality include hypothesis tests, ANOVA, and regression.

- To deal with data with this kind of distribution, you may need to transform it.

COMMON SHAPES OF FREQUENCY PLOTS: 4

Basically flat

If a frequency plot shows a basically flat distribution:
- **Conclude** — Process may be "drifting" over time or process may be a mix of many operating conditions.
- **Action** — Use time plots to track over time; look for possible stratifying factors; standardize the process.

COMMON SHAPES OF FREQUENCY PLOTS: 5

One or more outliers

If a frequency plot shows one or more outliers:

- **Conclude** — Outlier data points are likely the result of clerical error or something unusual happening in the process.
- **Action** — Confirm outliers are not clerical error; treat like a special cause.

COMMON SHAPES OF FREQUENCY PLOTS: 6

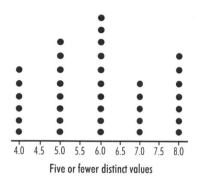

Five or fewer distinct values

If a frequency plot shows five or fewer distinct values:
- **Conclude** — Measuring device not sensitive enough or the measurement scale is not fine enough.
- **Action** — Fine tune measurements by recording additional decimal points.

COMMON SHAPES OF FREQUENCY PLOTS: 7

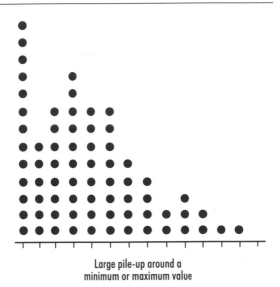

Large pile-up around a
minimum or maximum value

If a frequency plot shows a large pile-up of data points:
- **Conclude** — A sharp cut-off point occurs if the measurement instrument is incapable of reading across the complete range of data, or when people ignore data that goes beyond a certain limit.
- **Action** — Improve measurement devices. Eliminate fear of reprisals for recording "unacceptable" data.

COMMON SHAPES OF FREQUENCY PLOTS: 8

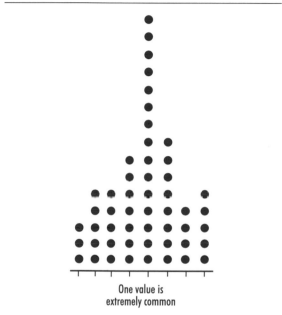

One value is
extremely common

If a frequency plot has one value that is extremely common:

- **Conclude** — When one value appears far more commonly than any other value, the measuring instrument may be damaged or hard to read, or the person recording the data may have a subconscious bias.

- **Action** — Check measurement instruments. Check data collection procedures.

COMMON SHAPES OF FREQUENCY PLOTS: 9

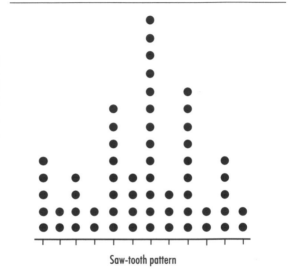

Saw-tooth pattern

If a frequency plot shows a saw-tooth pattern:
- **Conclude** — When data appear in alternating heights, the recorder may have a subconscious bias for even (or odd) numbers, the measuring instrument may be easier to read at odd or even numbers, or the data values may be rounded incorrectly.
- **Action** — Check measuring instrument and procedures.

Histograms are better for large data sets, say n > 50.

Dotplots are useful for small or large data sets.

PARETO CHARTS

Many times you have data that can best be analyzed by dividing it into categories. A **Pareto chart** is one of the best tools for looking at categorical data.

Why use a Pareto chart?
- Understanding the pattern of occurrence for a problem
- Judging the relative impact of various parts of a problem (quantifying the problem)
- Tracking down the biggest contributors to a problem
- Deciding where to focus efforts

When to use a Pareto chart
- The problem under study can be broken down into categories.
- You want to identify the "vital few" categories to focus your improvement effort.

Pareto chart features
- Used for categorical data
- Height of bar represents relative importance of that aspect of the problem.
- Bars are arranged in descending order from left to right.
- The bar for the biggest problem is always on the left.
- Height of vertical axis represents sum of all occurrences (not just the height of the tallest bar).

SAMPLE PARETO CHART

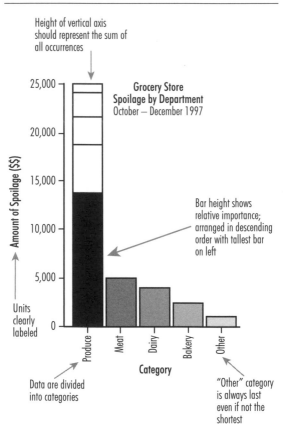

Height of vertical axis should represent the sum of all occurrences

**Grocery Store
Spoilage by Department**
October – December 1997

Amount of Spoilage ($$)

25,000

20,000

15,000

10,000

5,000

0

Bar height shows relative importance; arranged in descending order with tallest bar on left

Units clearly labeled

Produce

Meat

Dairy

Bakery

Other

Category

Data are divided into categories

"Other" category is always last even if not the shortest

How to construct a Pareto chart

1. Decide which problem you want to know more about.

2. Gather the necessary data.

3. Compare the relative frequency (or cost) of each problem category.

4. List the problem categories (sorted by frequency, in descending order) on the horizontal line and frequencies on the vertical line.

5. Draw the cumulative percentage line showing the portion of the total that each problem category represents (optional).

6. Interpret the results.

What to look for

- Relative heights of the bars (including height of the Y-axis) — make sure the Pareto Principle applies

- Size of the Other category — make sure you can't make another category from some of the "Other" data

- Type of data used to create the chart — is the chart based on valid data?

The Pareto Principle implies that we can frequently solve a problem by identifying and attacking its "vital few" sources.

React to a Pareto chart when the Pareto Principle holds; i.e., a few categories are responsible for most of the problem.

Reaction

- Begin work on the largest bar(s).

- When you've narrowed down the problem, continue to **Phase 3: Analyzing Causes**.

When the Pareto Principle does not hold

When all the bars are roughly the same height and/or many categories are needed to account for most of the problem, you need to find another way to look at the data.

PROCESS CAPABILITY

Process capability measures are statistical measures that summarize how much variation there is in a process relative to customer specifications.

Uses of Process Capability Indices:

- Provides management with a single number to assess the performance of a process.
- Provides a scale by which processes can be compared. You can state that process X is more capable than process Y if the capability index for process X is greater than the capability index for process Y. Such comparison can help prioritize improvement efforts.
- Shows over time whether a particular process is better able to meet specifications.

To increase process capability, you have to decrease the process variation. Less variation provides:

- Greater predictability in the process, allowing us to make reliable forecasts, meet schedules for orders, etc.
- Less waste and rework, which lowers costs
- Products and services that perform better and last longer
- Happier customers

UNDERSTANDING PROCESS CAPABILITY

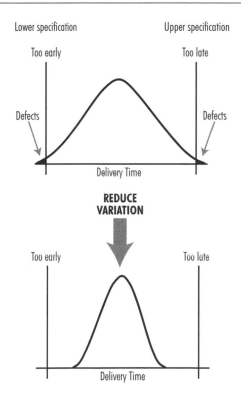

PROCESS SIGMA

Process Sigma builds on the basic foundation of process data and specification limits.

While process sigma shares some features with process capability indices, process sigma may also be applied to:

- Any situation where you can count the defects in meeting customer specifications.
- Multistep processes, in case you want an overall measure of process performance.

The process sigma scale is below.

DPMO	Process Sigma
308,537	2
66,807	3
6,210	4
233	5
3.4	6
Defects per million opportunities	Process Capability

Increase in Process Sigma requires exponential defect reduction →

(distribution shifted $\pm\,1.5\sigma$)

The preferred, standard method of determining **DPMO** (**D**efects **P**er **M**illion **O**pportunities) is to use **actual process data** and count how many defect opportunities are outside the specification limits — then **scale that number up** to the equivalent of a million opportunities.

Why use process sigma as a metric?
- It is a more sensitive indicator than percentage
- It focuses on defects

Even one defect reflects a failure in your customer's eyes.

Percent	DPMO	Process Sigma
93%	66,807	3.0
98%	22,750	3.5
99.4%	6,210	4.0
99 87%	1,350	4.5
99.977%	233	5.0
99.9997%	3.4	6.0

Determining Process Sigma
- Process Sigma is the capability of the process relative to specifications for that process.
- In practice, you determine yield for each step, then combine those yields to determine overall process sigma.
- To determine yields, you will need to know what a defect is and a defect opportunity.

Terminology

- **Process Sigma** = An expression of process yield (based on the number of defects per million opportunities — DPMO)
- **Unit** = The item produced or processed
- **CTQ** = **C**ritical **T**o **Q**uality
- **Defect** = Any event that does not meet a customer specification
  - A defect must be measurable
- **Defect Opportunity** = A measurable chance for a defect to occur
- **Defective** = A unit with one or more defects

Defect Opportunities

- An **opportunity** occurs each time the product, service, or information is handled, the point at which a customer quality requirement is either met or missed.
- **Defect opportunities** counts the number of times a requirement could be missed, **not** the ways in which it is missed.
- Number of opportunities per unit must **stay constant** before and after improvement.
- An opportunity should be based on a defect that can reasonably happen. If something has never been a problem, don't count it as an opportunity.
  - Inflating the number of opportunities will artificially inflate the sigma level.
- The number of defect opportunities should bear some relation to the complexity of the value-added process — that is, more complex processes should have more opportunities than simple ones.

©2002 Rath & Strong/Aon Management Consulting

Definitions are critical

Apply the concept of Operational Definitions to both defects and opportunities. Make sure everyone who works with sigma values understands and agrees on critical definitions.

- Defects: Focus on customer requirements.
- Clearly specify what is an opportunity so that all involved understand the definition.

THE SIGMA TABLE

Sigma	DPMO	Yield	Sigma	DPMO	Yield
6	3.4	99.99966%	2.9	80,757	91.9%
5.9	5.4	99.99946%	2.8	96,801	90.3%
5.8	8.5	99.99915%	2.7	115,070	88.5%
5.7	13	99.99866%	2.6	135,666	86.4%
5.6	21	99.99979%	2.5	158,655	84.1%
5.5	32	99.9968%	2.4	184,060	81.6%
5.4	48	99.9952%	2.3	211,855	78.8%
5.3	72	99.99928%	2.2	241,964	75.8%
5.2	108	99.9892%	2.1	274,253	72.6%
5.1	159	99.984%	2	308,538	69.1%
5	233	99.977%	1.9	344,578	65.5%
4.9	337	99.966%	1.8	382,089	61.8%
4.8	483	99.952%	1.7	420,740	57.9%
4.7	687	99.931%	1.6	460,172	54.0%
4.6	968	99.90%	1.5	500,000	50.0%
4.5	1,350	99.87%	1.4	539,828	46.0%
4.4	1,866	99.81%	1.3	579,260	42.1%
4.3	2,555	99.74%	1.2	617,911	38.2%
4.2	3,467	99.65%	1.1	655,422	34.5%
4.1	4,661	99.53%	1	691,462	30.9%
4	6,210	99.38%	0.9	725,747	27.4%
3.9	8,198	99.18%	0.8	758,036	24.2%
3.8	10,724	98.9%	0.7	788,145	21.2%
3.7	13,903	98.6%	0.6	815,940	18.4%
3.6	17,864	98.2%	0.5	841,345	15.9%
3.5	22,750	97.7%	0.4	864,334	13.6%
3.4	28,716	97.1%	0.3	884,930	11.5%
3.3	35,930	96.4%	0.2	903,199	9.7%
3.2	44,565	95.5%	0.1	919,243	8.1%
3.1	54,799	94.5%			
3	66,807	93.3%			

COMPLETION CHECKLIST

Before moving on to Phase 3: **Analyze**, you should be able to precisely define what problems are occurring and under what conditions they are likely to appear. You should have data in hand that you can use to demonstrate to your sponsor:

- What specifically is the main problem or problems.
- How you prioritized and selected critical input, process and output measures.
- What you have done to validate the measurement system.
- What patterns are exhibited in the data.
- What the current process capability is.

Phase 3: ANALYZE

The **Measure** phase has produced the baseline performance of the process. By having stratified the data in the baseline performance, it became possible to pinpoint the location or source of problems by building a factual understanding of existing process conditions and problems. That helps to focus the problem statement. In the **Analyze** phase you will develop theories of root causes, confirm the theories with data, and finally identify the root cause(s) of the problem. The verified cause(s) will form the basis for solutions in the next phase.

The tools used most commonly in the Analyze phase are:
1. Affinity Diagrams (covered in the Define phase)
2. Brainstorming
3. Cause-and-Effect Diagrams
4. Control Charts (covered in the Measure and Control phases)
5. Data Collection Forms (covered in the Measure phase)
6. Data Collection Plan (covered in the Measure phase)

7. Design of Experiments
8. Flow Diagrams
9. Frequency Plots (covered in the Measure phase)
10. Hypothesis Tests
11. Pareto Chart (covered in the Measure phase)
12. Regression Analysis
13. Response Surface Methodology
14. Sampling (covered in the Measure phase)
15. Scatter Plots
16. Stratified Frequency Plots

ORGANIZING POTENTIAL CAUSES

Once the problem has been focused, the team will create a list of potential causes and then organize those causes in order to see relationships between cause and effect. An underlying assumption of many of the tools used in the Analyze phase is that the data roughly fit a normal distribution. It might be necessary to transform data that do not fit a normal distribution. Causes are verified so that improvements focus on the deep cause, not on the original symptom.

It is time to generate a lot of potential causes, organize them, and decide which potential causes to verify.

BRAINSTORMING

In the Analyze phase, brainstorming is used to generate a lot of ideas quickly to identify potential causes. Brainstorming encourages creativity, involves everyone, generates excitement and energy, and separates people from the ideas they suggest.

Brainstorming Methods
- Rounds — Go around in turn, one item per turn, until everyone passes.

©2002 Rath & Strong/Aon Management Consulting

- Popcorn — Anyone calls out ideas, no order, until all ideas are out.

Guidelines
- Start with silent "think" time
- Freewheel — don't hold back
- NO CRITICISM
- Hitchhike — build upon ideas
- The more ideas, the better
- Post ideas

THE FIVE WHYS

To push for root causes, start with the focused problem statement and then ask why five times. An example of a problem statement is, "customers complain about waiting too long to get connected to staff during lunch hours."

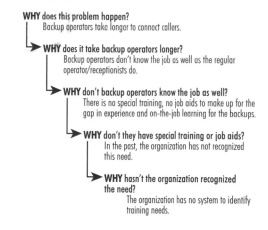

WHY does this problem happen?
Backup operators take longer to connect callers.

WHY does it take backup operators longer?
Backup operators don't know the job as well as the regular operator/receptionists do.

WHY don't backup operators know the job as well?
There is no special training, no job aids to make up for the gap in experience and on-the-job learning for the backups.

WHY don't they have special training or job aids?
In the past, the organization has not recognized this need.

WHY hasn't the organization recognized the need?
The organization has no system to identify training needs.

Graphic displays can help you structure possible causes in order to find relationships that will shed new light on the problem. Most people have had the experience of "solving" a problem over and over again — meaning the actions taken really didn't get to the root of the problem. Use of cause-and-effect and tree diagrams can help make your solutions more effective the first time around by making sure you uncover deep causes to a problem.

CAUSE-AND-EFFECT DIAGRAM

Cause-and-effect diagrams graphically display potential causes of a problem. The layout shows cause-and-effect relationships between the potential causes.

Why use cause-and-effect diagrams

- To stimulate thinking during a brainstorm of potential causes.
- To understand relationships between potential causes.
- To track which potential causes have been investigated, and which proved to contribute significantly to the problem.

It is common for people working on improvement efforts to jump to conclusions without studying the causes, target one possible cause while ignoring others, and take actions aimed at surface symptoms. Cause-and-effect diagrams are designed to help circumvent these natural tendencies by:

- Providing a structure to understand the relationships between many possible causes of a problem.
- Giving people a framework for planning what data to collect.
- Serving as a visual display of causes that have been studied.
- Helping team members communicate within the team and with the rest of the organization.

CAUSE-AND-EFFECT DIAGRAM FEATURES

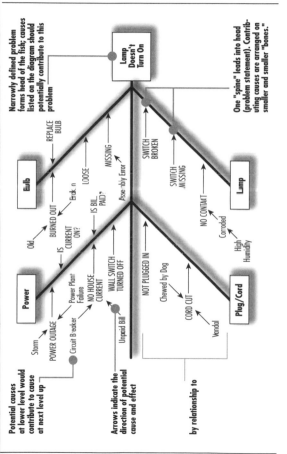

Narrowly defined problem forms head of the fish; causes listed on the diagram should potentially contribute to this problem

One "spine" leads into head (problem statement). Contributing causes are arranged on smaller and smaller "bones."

Lamp Doesn't Turn On

Bulb

REPLACE BULB

MISSING

LOOSE

Erak n

BURNED OUT

Old

IS CURRENT ON?

IS BIL PAD*

Assembly Error

SWITCH BROKEN

SWITCH MISSING

Lamp

NO CONTACT

Corroded

High Humidity

Power

Storm

POWER OUTAGE

Circuit Breaker

Power Plant Failure

NO HOUSE CURRENT

Unpaid Bill

WALL SWITCH TURNED OFF

NOT PLUGGED IN

Chewed by Dog

CORD CUT

Vandal

Plug/Cord

Potential causes at lower level would contribute to cause at next level up

Arrows indicate the direction of potential cause and effect

by relationship to

When to use cause-and-effect diagrams

1. A large number of potential causes makes it difficult to focus the analysis.
2. There is lack of clarity about the relationship between different potential causes.

How to construct a cause-and-effect diagram

1. Review the Focused Problem Statement.
2. Identify possible causes.
3. Sort possible causes into reasonable clusters.
4. Choose a cluster and label a main bone.
5. Develop and arrange bones for that cluster.
6. Develop other main bones.
7. Add title, date, and contact person.
8. Select possible causes to verify with data.

VERIFYING CAUSES

A lot of thinking and effort goes into constructing a cause-and-effect diagram. But such diagrams only identify potential causes. You need to collect data to confirm which potential causes actually contribute to the problem.

Which causes to verify

- You likely identified many potential causes on your cause-and-effect diagram or other tool.
- Now you need to set priorities and collect data on only the most likely causes.
- Mark on the diagram which potential causes you want to verify.

In order to set priorities you should:

- Review all the potential causes

- Identify which are the most likely contributors to the problem.
- Consider how measurable each of these likely contributors are.
- Consider which of the causes you should take action on.
- If these considerations don't help you narrow the list significantly, have each team member vote on the top two or three choices.

In general, it pays to focus on the causes you can most easily collect data on. However, some important causes may be hard to measure or observe, and you may need to be creative in coming up with ways to get data on those causes. Often, performing a simple experiment — where you change the targeted factor and observe the effect — will do the trick.

Knowing which potential causes you could really change will also help you focus your efforts. It doesn't help to put a lot of effort into gathering data on something you have no control over.

Testing a theory with data
- The potential cause is really a theory that two factors — a cause and an effect — are related.
- You need data to verify whether the cause-and-effect relationship truly exists.
- You can analyze existing data to test that theory, or collect new data.

Analyzing cause-and-effect data
The type of data you have or will collect determines what tools you can use.
- Scatter Plots
- Frequency Plots
- Tables of Results

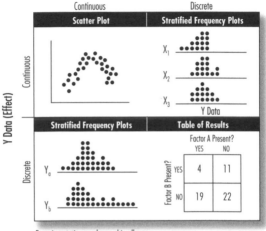

Experimentation can be used in all cases.

The Focus of the Analyze phase: $Y = f(X_1, X_2, X_3...X_n)$ where Y is the output or effect and the Xs are the input and process variables that drive Y. The main question to be answered in the Analyze phase is, "What vital few process and input variables affect critical-to-quality process performance or output measures?"

Process or Data Door

It is recommended to go through both doors to make sure that potential causes are not overlooked.

Process Door — Detailed Process Maps, Value Added Analysis, Cycle Time Analysis
  · To improve the understanding of process flow

- To tackle cycle-time problems
- To identify opportunities to reduce process costs

Data Door — Stratification, Scatter Diagrams, Multi-vari Plots
- To understand the drivers of variation in the process
- To tackle quality problems and waste
- To understand the root cause of differences between outputs

PROCESS DOOR

Flow Diagrams
Flow diagrams are graphical displays that make a process visible.

Why use flow diagrams?
- To create a common understanding
- To clarify the steps in a process
- To identify improvement opportunities in a process (complexity, waste, delays, inefficiencies and bottlenecks)
- To uncover problems in the process
- To reveal how the process operates

When to use flow diagrams
- To create a common understanding
- To clarify the steps in a process
- To build consensus on how a process actually operates and how it should operate
- To understand the cause of common problems with how all units are processed

TYPES OF FLOW DIAGRAMS

Basic or high-level flow diagram (as seen in SIPOC)

Activity flow diagrams

These are specific about what happens in a process. They often
capture decision points, rework loops, complexity, etc.

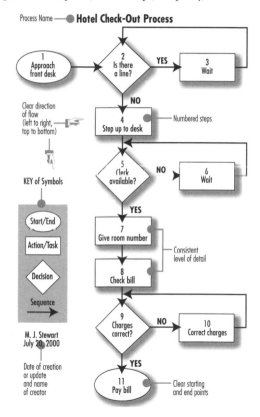

Deployment flow diagrams
These show the detailed steps in a process and which people or groups are involved in each step.

INVOICING PROCESS

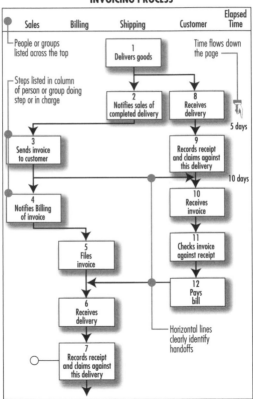

©2002 Rath & Strong/Aon Management Consulting

Which flow diagramming technique should I use?

Basic Flowchart	Activity Flowchart	Deployment Flowchart
• To identify the major steps of the process and where it begins and ends • To illustrate where in the process you will collect data	• To display the complexity and decision points of a process • To identify rework loops and bottlenecks	• To help highlight handoff areas in processes between people or functions • To clarify roles and indicate dependencies

How to create a flow diagram

When creating a flowchart, work with a group so you can get multiple viewpoints.

- Brainstorm action steps.
  - Write these on self-stick notes or on a flipchart.
  - Make sure you include the steps that occur when things go wrong.
- Arrange the steps in sequence.
  - Be consistent in the direction of flow — time should always flow from top to bottom, or from left to right.
  - Use appropriate flowchart symbols.
- Check for missing steps or decision points.
- Number the steps.

VALUE-ADDED AND NON-VALUE-ADDED STEPS

Value-added steps
- Customers are willing to pay for it.
- It physically changes the product.
- It's done right the first time.

Non-value-added steps
- Are not essential to produce output.
- Do not add value to the output.
- Include:
  - Defects, errors, omissions
  - Preparation/setup, control/inspection
  - Over-production, processing, inventory
  - Transporting, motion, waiting, delays

OPPORTUNITY FLOW DIAGRAM

Organized to separate value-added steps from non-value-added steps.

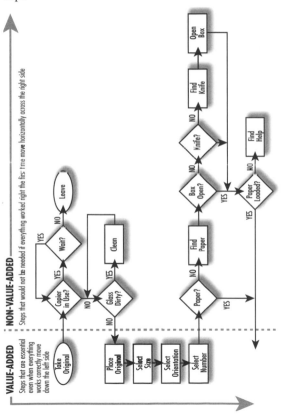

NON-VALUE-ADDED
Steps that would not be needed if everything worked right the first time move horizontally across the right side

VALUE-ADDED
Steps that are essential even when everything works correctly move down the left side

CYCLE-TIME REDUCTION

Understanding cycle time
- Provides a better understanding of the process
- Shows the impact of non-value-added steps on the time to produce product or service
- Identifies bottlenecks in the process

Reducing cycle time
- Helps increase predictability in the process
- Helps reduce waste and rework, which reduces costs
- Provides a competitive advantage by reducing cycle time

When analyzing cycle time, focus on the "thing," not the people.

Process analysis review
- Create an activity or deployment flowchart to map out the steps.
- Use opportunity flowcharts or other approaches to identify waste and complexity.
- Measure cycle time so you can calculate both value-added and non-value-added time.
- Identify bottlenecks:
  - Any resource whose capacity limits the amount of information or material that flows through the process
  - Any resource whose capacity is equal to or less than the demand placed upon it

DATA DOOR

Stratified Frequency Plots

When one variable has continuous data and another has attribute or discrete data, the best option for analyzing results is stratified frequency plots.

- Gather continuous data for each of the attribute types or categories.
  - Collect data on number of defects for each of four different types of customized orders.
- Create a frequency plot for each category.
  - Use the same numeric scale and plot size for each plot so you can easily compare multiple plots.
- Look for patterns.

Discrete X and Continuous Y

Theory — Variation in training, technique, and procedures at different locations accounts for much of the variation in how long it takes to complete oil change/lubes.

Data — Measure time needed to complete lube job at different locations.

Cause (X) = discrete data (location).

Effect (Y) = continuous data on time needed to complete oil change/lube.

In this example, the lubes done at Location B are generally faster than those at either Location A or Location C. The next step for this company would be to see if they can discover the cause for these differences.

DISCRETE X AND CONTINUOUS Y

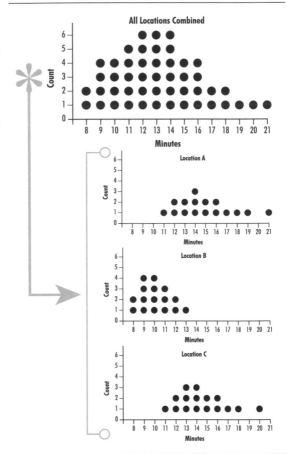

CONTINUOUS X AND DISCRETE Y

Theory — The more time spent with a customer, the more likely we will make a sale.

Data — Measure the time spent with the customer and separate it into two categories (Made the Sale *vs.* Did Not Make the Sale).

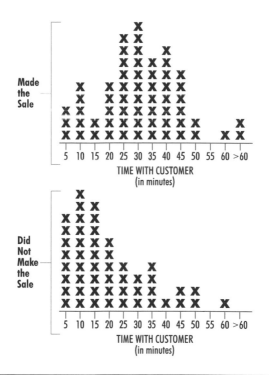

This example shows that most sales were made when the sales representative spent 25 to 45 minutes with the customer. Most non-sales occurred when the sales rep spent 20 minutes or less with the customer.

SCATTER PLOTS

A **scatter plot** is a graph that helps you visualize the relationship between two variables. It can be used to check whether one variable is related to another variable and is an effective way to communicate the relationship you find.

Why use scatter plots?
- Studying and identifying possible relationships between the changes observed in two different sets of variables
- Understanding relationships between variables

When to use scatter plots
- To discover whether two variables are related
- To find out if changes in one variable are associated with changes in the other
- To test for a cause-and-effect relationship (but finding a relationship does not always imply causation)

SCATTER PLOT FEATURES

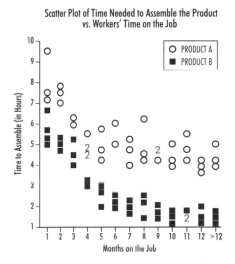

Scatter Plot of Time Needed to Assemble the Product
vs. Workers' Time on the Job

Each data point represents a pair of measurements (e.g., 8 hours
after 2 months on the job)

Two variables are represented. Often the effect is on the vertical axis
and the potential cause is on the horizontal axis

Both axes are roughly equal in length, so the plot is square

The pattern formed by the scatter is an important clue to how the two
variables are related

Stratification using different symbols allows you to look at multiple
patterns at once

How to create a scatter plot

1. Collect paired data along with other information. Other information includes potential stratification factors.

2. Determine which variable will be on the horizontal axis (x) and which will be on the vertical (y). By convention, place the potential cause on the horizontal axis and the effect on the vertical axis.

3. Find the minimum and maximum of x and y.

4. Set up the plot axes. The axes should be the same length.

5. Plot all the x, y pairs on the graph.

6. Label the graph.

Interpreting a scatter plot

· Look for outliers.

· Interpret the pattern formed by the scatter of the data points.

SCATTER PLOT PATTERNS

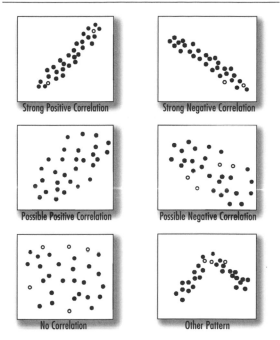

The tighter together the points are clustered, the stronger the correlation.

A pattern that slopes from the lower left to the upper right means that as the variable on the X-axis increases, so does the variable on the Y-axis. This is a positive correlation. A scatter plot of the number of paper jams in the copier *vs.* the humidity might show a positive correlation because as the humidity goes up the number of paper jams also increases.

A pattern that slopes from the upper left to the lower right means that as the variable on the X-axis increases, the variable on the Y-axis decreases. This is a negative correlation. A scatter plot of the order lead time vs. the number of operators in the shift might show a negative correlation because as the number of operators goes up, the lead time goes down.

Correlation and Causation

Even strong correlations do not imply causation. Just because there is a pattern on the scatter plot, it doesn't mean the two variables are related. For example, there will likely be a positive correlation — but not causation — between the occurrence of vapor-locks in automobiles and the use of public swimming pools. On the other hand, no correlation does not mean there is no causation. There may be relationships over a wider range of data, or a different portion of the range.

Verify cause review

· Select the most likely causes to verify.

· Use existing data or collect new data to see if these causes contribute to the problem.

· Use scatter plots, stratified frequency plots, tables, or experimentation to understand the relationship between causes and effects.

HYPOTHESIS TESTS

A hypothesis test is a procedure that summarizes data so you can detect differences among groups. It is used to make comparisons between two or more groups.

Type of Data	What You Can Compare	Example
Discrete	Proportions	Is the % on-time deliveries for Supplier A the same as for Supplier B?
Continuous	Averages	Is the average production volume the same for all three shifts?
	Variation	Do results from the group using the New Method vary less than the results from the group using the Old Method?
	Shapes or Distributions	How does the distribution of cycle time compare for various methods?

How hypothesis tests work

Because of variation, no two anythings will be exactly alike.

The question is whether differences you see between samples, groups, processes, etc., **are due to random, common-cause variation, or if there is a real difference**.

To help us make this decision, various hypothesis tests provide ways of estimating common cause variation for different situations.

They test whether a difference is significantly bigger than the common cause variation we would expect for the situation.

If the answer is no, there is no statistical evidence of a difference. If the answer is yes, conclude the groups are significantly different.

Hypothesis tests take advantage of larger samples because the variation among averages decreases as the sample size increases.

A hypothesis test:
- Tests the **null** hypothesis
  - H_0: no difference between groups
- Against the **alternative** hypothesis
  - H_a: groups are different
- Obtain a P-value for the null hypothesis.
- Use the data and the appropriate hypothesis; test statistic to obtain a P-value.
- If P is less than .05, reject the H_0 and conclude the H_a.
- If P greater than or equal to .05, cannot reject the H_0.

Why use hypothesis tests?
- To detect differences that may be important to the business.
- You wonder if minor difference in averages is due to random variation or if it reflects a true difference.

When to use a hypothesis test
- When you need to compare two or more groups
  - On average
  - In variability
  - In proportion
- You are not sure if a true difference exists

Assumptions for hypothesis tests
If data are continuous, we assume the underlying distribution is Normal.

You may need to transform non-Normal data (such as cycle times).

When comparing groups from different populations we assume:
  · Independent samples
  · Achieved through random sampling
  · The samples are representative (unbiased) of the population.

When comparing groups from different processes we assume:
  · Each process is stable.
  · There are no special causes or shifts over time (that is, no time-related differences).
  · The samples are representative of the process (unbiased).

P-value definitions
  · Hypothesis tests compare observed differences between groups.
  · The P-value equals the probability of obtaining the observed difference given that the "true" difference is zero (= the null hypothesis).
  · P-values range from 0.0 to 1.0 (0% chance to 100% chance).
  · By convention, usually treat P as less than .05 as indicative that the difference is significant.
  · If P is less than .05, conclude there is little chance that the true difference is 0.

TYPES OF HYPOTHESIS TESTS

Hypothesis Test	Purpose
t-test	Compare two group averages
Paired t-test	Compare two group averages when data is matched
ANOVA (F-test) (Analysis of Variance)	Compare two or more group averages Compare two or more group variances
Chi-Square test	Compare two or more group proportions

WHICH ANALYSIS METHOD DO I USE?

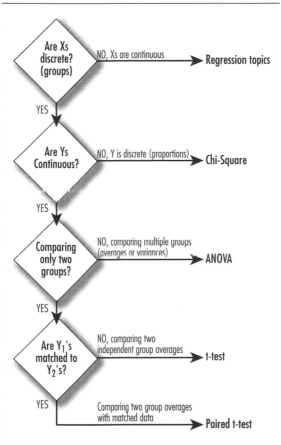

How to use a hypothesis test
1. Determine the type of test suited to your data and question.
2. Select the appropriate test.
3. Obtain p value; declare statistically significant difference if $p < .05$.

Two types of errors in hypothesis testing
There are four possible outcomes to any decision we make based on a hypothesis test: We can decide the groups are the same or different, and we can be right or wrong.

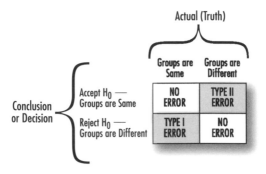

Type I error — Deciding the groups are different when they aren't (the difference is due to random variation).

Type II error — Not detecting a difference when there really is one.

P-value = the probability of making a Type I error (deciding the groups are different when they really aren't)

You choose what level of Type I error you're willing to live with; by convention, it is usually set at .05 (= 5% chance).

The probability of making a Type II error can be calculated given an assumed true difference.

Practical implications of type I and type II errors
· Both errors are important.
· Guarding too heavily against one error increases the risk of the other error.
· Increasing the sample size
· Reduces the risk of Type II errors
· Allows you to detect smaller differences

T-TEST
We use a statistical test called the **t-test** for comparing and judging differences between two group averages:

$$t_{(\bar{A} - \bar{B})} = \frac{(\overline{X}_A - \overline{X}_D) - 0}{S_{(\bar{A} - \bar{B})}}$$

The formula for t is the same as for Z, but P-values are obtained from the t-distribution instead of the Z-distribution.

The confidence interval
A 95% confidence interval is the range of values we expect to contain the true difference between the two group averages.

It's based on the "difference distribution of averages," not the differences between individual observations.

It does not represent the range of values we expect for the difference between individual growth times; that range would be wider.

If there is no significant difference between the group averages, the confidence interval will contain 0 (that is, range from negative [−] to positive [+]).

Summary of the t-test
- It is a test of hypothesis for comparing two averages.
- The hypothesis is that the two group averages are the same.
- Their difference = 0.
- If P-value is low, reject the hypothesis.
- By convention, a P-value is considered low if it is < .05.

Common notation

Null hypothesis	H_0: mean$_A$ = mean$_B$
Alternative hypothesis	H_a: mean$_A$ ≠ mean$_B$

PAIRED T-TEST
Matched or paired data

Two measurements are obtained for each **sampling unit** (a transaction, phone call, employee, deal, application, etc.). Measurements in the second group are not independent from those in the first group. They are **matched or paired**. The second measurements are taken on the **same sampling units** as the first measurements.

Practical implications of Paired t-test
- The Paired t-test is a powerful way to compare two methods.
- *Requires a special matched data structure*. The sampling unit (a machine, an operation, an employee, a piece of material, etc.):
  – Has each method applied to it
  – With little or no carryover from the use of the first method to the use of the second
  – Requires planning
  – Applies in the analysis or improvement stages of a project

---

126

   – For example, you're seeking to find or demonstrate a difference between two ways of running a process.

ANOVA
Comparing two or more group averages.

ANOVA is a statistical test that uses variances to compare multiple averages simultaneously. Instead of comparing pair wise averages, it compares the variance between groups to the variance within groups.

The between-group variance is obtained from the variance, s^2, of the **group averages**. The within-group variance is obtained from the variance, s^2, among values within each group, and then **pooled** (or averaged with appropriate dfs) **across the groups**.

If the variance between groups is the same as the variance within groups, we say there is no difference between the group averages.

$$\frac{S^2_{between}}{S^2_{within}}$$

- Obtain the variance between groups.
- Obtain the variance within groups.
- If they are about the same, conclude there is no significant difference between groups.
- The ratio of two variances = F-statistic.
- We get a P-value from the F-distribution.

Assumptions for ANOVA
- The samples are representative of the population or process.
- The process is stable.

- Only common causes of variation are at work on the process.
- No shifts or trends over time (no time-related special causes).
- The variance for each group is the same.
- Can be verified with the F-test .
- Violation of these assumptions can cause incorrect conclusions in the ANOVA analysis.
- It is also assumed that the underlying distribution of each group is Normal. This can be checked with a Normal probability plot of residuals, which is discussed in the Regression section.

Does the variation differ between groups? How to check.
There is a statistical test called **Homogeneity of Variance** to check this assumption. "Homogeneity" means "the same"— so you're testing if the variances are the same.

Review of ANOVA
- Used to compare averages of two or more groups
- Assumes variances of each group are the same
- Also used to compare variances of two or more groups
- Called the Homogeneity of Variance test
- Use this test to check the assumption that variances are the same when comparing averages.

CHI-SQUARE

This is the hypothesis test used to compare two or more group proportions. It is used when both X and Y are discrete. The counts are summarized in a table known as a contingency table. The Chi-Square measures the difference between the observed and expected counts in this way:

$$x^2 = \sum \frac{(\text{Observed} - \text{Expected})^2}{\text{Expected}}$$

What next?

Determine which group proportions are different.

Determine why the group proportions are different.

Assumptions of the Chi-Square Test

· The sample is representative of the population or process.

· We assume the underlying distribution is binomial for discrete data used in a x^2 test.

· The expected count greater than or equal to 5 for each cell, or the test will not perform properly.

· If expected count is less than 5, collecting additional data (a bigger sample size) may be needed.

Value of Chi-Square Test

· Discrete data are commonly collected and used to analyze process performance in the service applications within manufacturing.

· Non-significant differences between two or more groups keep you from chasing ghosts.

· There is little to gain by studying the best or trying to motivate the worst performers.

· Significant differences between group proportions can be detected.

· A low P-value (less than .05) indicates that it is appropriate to identify root causes that might lead to significant differences between groups.

· Examine the chi-square values for each cell to determine which groups are different.

• Remember to consider whether the size of the "statistically significant" difference in proportions is actually important to the business.

REGRESSION ANALYSIS

Regression analysis generates a line that quantifies the relationship between X and Y. The line, or **regression equation**, is represented as $Y = b_0 + b_1X$, where

b_0 = **intercept** (where the line crosses X = 0);

b_1 = **slope** (rise over run, or change in Y per unit increase in X).

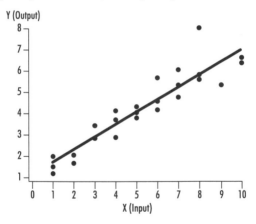

Benefits of quantifying a relationship
• Prediction
  – The equation can be used to predict future Ys by plugging in an X-value.

- Control
  - If X is controllable, you can manipulate process conditions to avoid undesirable results and/or generate desirable results.

Extrapolation is making predictions outside the range of the X data. It is a natural desire, but it is like walking from solid ground onto thin ice. Predictions from regression equations are more reliable for Xs within the range of observed data.

A residual is the vertical distance from each point to the regression line. It equals Observed Y minus Predicted Y. It is the leftover variation in Y after using X to predict Y.

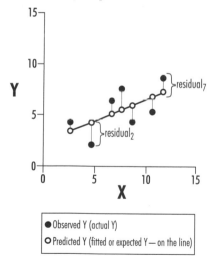

● Observed Y (actual Y)

○ Predicted Y (fitted or expected Y — on the line)

The least squares method

The regression equation is determined by a procedure that minimizes the total squared distance of all points to the line.

- Finds the line where the squared vertical distance from each data point to the line is as small as possible (or the "least")

- Restated...minimizes the "square" of all the residuals

- Regression uses the least squares method to determine the "best line":

  – Data (both X and Y values) are used to obtain b_0 and b_1 values.

  – The b_0 and b_1 values establish the equation.

TYPES OF REGRESSION

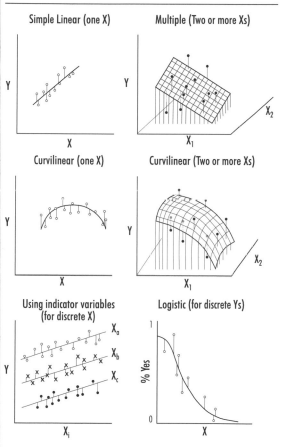

Simple Linear (one X)

Multiple (Two or more Xs)

Curvilinear (one X)

Curvilinear (Two or more Xs)

Using indicator variables (for discrete X)

Logistic (for discrete Ys)

Assumptions of regression are based on properties of the residuals (not the original data). We assume residuals are:
- Not related to the Xs
- **Stable and independent**, do not change over time
- **Constant**, do not increase as predicted Ys increase
- **Normal** (bell-shaped) with mean of 0
- **Residuals *vs.* Each X** is used to check that the residuals are not related to the Xs.
  - If the relationship between X and Y is not a straight line, but a curve, try a transformation on X, Y, or both. Or use X_2 in a multiple regression.
- **Time Plot of Residuals** is used to check for stability over time.
  - Any pattern visible over time means another factor, related to time, influences Y. Try to discover it and include it in a multiple regression.
- **Residuals *vs.* Predicted Y (Fits)** is used to check that they are constant over the range of Ys.
  - A fan shape means the variation increases as Y gets larger (it's not constant). Try a square root, log, or inverse transformation on Y.
- **Normal Probability Plot of Residuals** is used to check that residuals are Normal.
  - If the residuals are not Normal, try a transformation on X or Y or both.

Confidence and Prediction Intervals
- **Confidence Interval** = An interval likely to contain the "best fit" line.

- Gives a range of the predicted values for the fitted Y if the regression is repeated again

- Is based on a given X-value for a given confidence

- **Prediction Interval** = An interval likely to contain the actual Y values for a given X.

- Gives a range of likely actual values for Y

- Based on a given X-value

- For a given Confidence interval

- A Confidence Interval, which is predicting how much the fitted line could vary, *will always be narrower than* a Prediction Interval, which accounts for variation of the individual values around the fitted line.

Name	Definition	Range	Meaning
P-value for slope	Probability that the slope is significant (different from zero)	0 to 1	If less than .05, the slope is significant (different from zero) and X is linearly related to Y.
r	Correlation coefficient	−1 to +1	Indicates the strength of a linear relationship. Numbers near zero indicate no linear relationship.
R-square (R-sq)	Percent of explained variation: = r^2	0 to 100%	% of variation in the Y-values explained by the linear relationship with X.
s	Standard deviation of the residuals (unexplained variation)	0 to ∞	Indicates how much the typical observed value differs from the fitted value, in units of the original data.
Residual	= Observed Y − Predicted Y	−∞ to +∞	Residuals are assumed to be random, and Normal with a mean of zero (represent common-cause variation).
Standardized Residual	$=\dfrac{\text{residual}}{\text{standard deviation}}$	About −3 to about +3	If the absolute value of a standardized residual is > 3, then it's an unusual observation. Investigate it.
Influential Observation	An observation whose X-value has a large influence on the values of the coefficients (the regression line)	−∞ to +∞	View them on a plot to decide whether you will keep them or drop them from the regression analysis.

DESIGN OF EXPERIMENTS

This is an approach for effectively and efficiently exploring the cause-and-effect relationship between numerous process variables (Xs) and the output or process performance variable (Y).

- Identifies the "vital few" sources of variation (Xs)
  - Those that have the biggest impact on results
- Quantifies the **effects** of the important Xs, including their interactions
- Produces an equation that quantifies the **relationship** between the Xs and Y
  - You can predict how much gain or loss will result from changes in process conditions.

Full Factorial

The Factorial Approach to Designed Experiments:

- Changes several factors (variables) simultaneously, not one-at-a-time
- Initially begins with only 2 conditions for each factor
- Considers **all possible combinations** of factor conditions
- May test all the combinations or a **carefully selected sub-set** of them
- Handles random (common-cause) variation easily and uses it to determine which factors are important
- Replication of trials (repeated testing of same combinations) is encouraged to help measure common-cause variation.
- Is easy to analyze
- Uses methods to deal with other factors not controlled in the experiment (such as randomization and blocking) so that conclusions are still valid

---

FULL FACTORIAL LAYOUT

Standard Order	Factor 1	Factor 2	Factor 3
1	–	–	–
2	+	–	–
3	–	+	–
4	+	+	–
5	–	–	+
6	+	–	+
7	–	+	+
8	+	+	+

A **full factorial** involves all possible combinations (later in the module we'll look at "fractional factorials" that involve a subset of all runs).

For 3 factors, each at 2 levels, there are 2 x 2 x 2 = 8 combinations of factor settings.

2 x 2 x 2 is often written as 2^3. The superscript 3 indicates the number of 2s multiplied together.

For 3 factors there are $2^3 = 8$ possible combinations of factor settings.

What is the pattern of factor settings in the standard order? (Hint: Look down the columns.)

Designing a full factorial experiment
Replication means repeating all the experimental conditions two or more times.

Why do replicates?
- To measure pure error: the amount of variability among runs performed at the same experimental conditions (this represents common cause variation)
- To see more clearly whether or not a factor is important — is the difference between responses due to a change in factor conditions (an induced special cause) or is it due to common cause variability?
- To see the effect of changing factor conditions not only on the average response, but also on response variability, if desired (two responses can be analyzed: the mean and the standard deviation.)

Randomization
Definition:
- To assign the order in which the experimental trials will be run using a random mechanism
- It is not the standard order.
- It is not running trials in an order that is convenient.
- To create a random order, you can "pull numbers from a hat" or have a computer randomize the sequence of trials for you

Why?
- Averages the effect of any lurking variables over all of the factors in the experiment
- Prevents the effect of a lurking variable from being mistakenly attributed to another factor
- Helps validate statistical conclusions made from the experiment

Analyzing the experiment

There are three phases of data analysis:

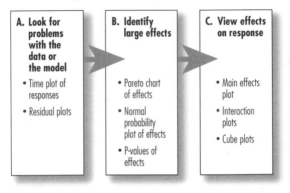

A. Look for problems with the data or the model
- Time plot of responses
- Residual plots

B. Identify large effects
- Pareto chart of effects
- Normal probability plot of effects
- P-values of effects

C. View effects on response
- Main effects plot
- Interaction plots
- Cube plots

Look for problems with the data.

1. Make a time plot of the response.
2. Interpret the plot by looking for:
   a. "Defects" in the data such as missing values, typos, etc.
   b. Trends or cycles that indicate lurking variables associated with time.

Residuals

Definition: Residual = (Observed Y) — (Average of Ys at that experimental condition)

A residual is the difference between a response and what we "expect" it to be (the expected value is the average of all replicates for a particular combination of factor settings).

- We hope most variation in the Ys is accounted for by deliberate changes we're making in the factor settings.

- Whatever variation is left over is residual.
  - The assumption is that this residual variation reflects the common cause-variation in the experiment.

Assumptions of DoE analysis

The Residuals: Residual = (Observed Y) − (Average at each experimental condition)

We assume the residuals are:
- Normal — bell-shaped with a mean of 0
- Constant — do not increase as averages of each experimental condition increase
- Stable — do not change over time
- Not related to the Xs (factors)
- Random — represent common causes of variation
- Independent

Residual plots must be checked to ensure the assumptions hold. Otherwise, conclusions may be incorrect or misleading.

Residuals Plot	Good	Bad	Meaning/Actions

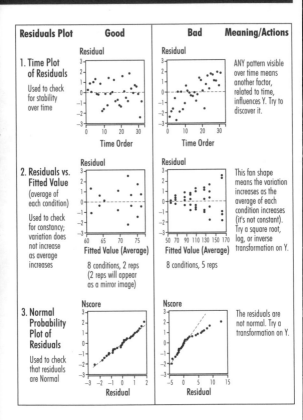

1. Time Plot of Residuals Used to check for stability over time	Residual Time Order	Residual Time Order	ANY pattern visible over time means another factor, related to time, influences Y. Try to discover it.
2. Residuals vs. Fitted Value (average of each condition) Used to check for constancy; variation does not increase as average increases	Residual Fitted Value (Average) 8 conditions, 2 reps (2 reps will appear as a mirror image)	Residual Fitted Value (Average) 8 conditions, 5 reps	This fan shape means the variation increases as the average of each condition increases (it's not constant). Try a square root, log, or inverse transformation on Y.
3. Normal Probability Plot of Residuals Used to check that residuals are Normal	Nscore Residual	Nscore Residual	The residuals are not normal. Try a transformation on Y.

Once you have verified that there are no problems with the data, you can look for factors that have the largest effect on the response. There are two types of effects, main effects and interaction effects.

The Main Effect
Definition — The main effect is the average increase (or decrease) in the response when moving from the low to the high level of a factor.

Formula for calculating main effects for each factor

$$\textbf{MAIN EFFECT} = \begin{pmatrix} \text{Average of all} \\ \text{observations at} \\ \text{High (+) level} \end{pmatrix} - \begin{pmatrix} \text{Average of all} \\ \text{observations at} \\ \text{Low (–) level} \end{pmatrix}$$

Interaction effects
Definition — An interaction occurs when the effect one factor has on the response (Y) is not the same for each level of another factor.

Formula for calculating the size of interaction effects:

$$\textbf{AB interaction} = \frac{\text{(Effect of A for high B)} - \text{(Effect of A for low B)}}{2}$$

Deciding which effects are large (significant)
There are three ways to decide which effects are large:
- P-value for each effect
- Pareto chart of effects
- Normal probability plot of effects

Drawing Conclusions
- List all your conclusions.

- Interpret the meaning of these results.
  - For example, relate them to known physical properties, engineering theories, or your own personal knowledge.
- Make recommendations.
- Formulate and write conclusions in simple language.

The prediction equation — using coefficients
Use the coefficients to generate an equation that lets you predict the response (Y) for various combinations.

For just one numerical factor, suppose the uncoded effect of A is .29.

The prediction equation for Y is Y = Constant + .29A.

Dropping terms from the prediction equation
Remove the insignificant terms. If an interaction is significant, it is standard practice to include the main effects of the factors involved, even if the main factors by themselves aren't significant.

Verify results
There are two key ways to verify the conclusions drawn from an experiment:
- **Confirmatory runs** — Run a few additional experiments at the recommended settings to see if the desired response is achieved.
- **Make actual recommended process changes** — Change the process and monitor it on a control chart to assure that the desired response is achieved and maintained.

Reducing experimental trials — the half-fraction and confounding
- In a full factorial design, information is available for all main effects (e.g., A, B, C).

©2002 Rath & Strong/Aon Management Consulting

- Interactions
  - Two-factor (e.g., AB, AC, BC)
  - Higher order interactions for three or more factors (e.g., ABC, ABCDE)
- When there are many factors, the number of higher-order interactions increases quickly.
- Higher-order interactions are usually negligible (involving more than 2 factors).
- There is a diminishing return of information on higher-order interactions; in general, the higher-order they are, the more negligible.

Cost/benefit of a half-fraction for 5 factors

Cost —
- Main effects and two-factor interactions are confounded with higher-order interactions.

Benefit —
- The number of runs is reduced by half.

REDUCED FRACTIONAL DESIGNS

The Knowledge Line is a strategy for choosing the appropriate design.

Current State of Process Knowledge

LOW ├────────┼────────┼────────┤ HIGH

	Screening	Fractional Factorials	Factorials	Response Surface
TYPE OF DESIGN	Screening	Fractional Factorials	Factorials	Response Surface
USUAL NO. OF FACTORS	>4	3 – 15	1 – 7	<8
PURPOSE: Identify	Most important factors (vital few)	Some interactions	Relationships among all factors	Optimal factor setting
PURPOSE: Estimate	Crude direction for improvement (linear effects)	All main effects and some interactions	All main effects and all interactions	Curvature in response, empirical models

Which approach to designed experiments you choose depends on how much you already know about a process and how many factors you want to test.

RESOLUTION: UNDERSTANDING THE DEGREE OF CONFOUNDING IN A FRACTIONAL FACTORIAL

RESOLUTION	INTERPETATION		COMMENTS
	Effect ...	Is Confounded With	
III	Main effects	2-factor and higher-order interactions	Main effects are clear of each other, but confounded with 2-way interactions.
	1 + 2 = 3		
IV	Main effects	3-factor and higher-order interactions	Main effects are clear of each other and clear of all 2-way interactions (so interpretation of main effects will not be affected if 2-way interactions are present).
	1 + 3 = 4		
	2-factor Interactions	Other 2-factor interactions and higher order intaractions	
	2 + 2 = 4		
V	Main effects	4-factor and higher-order interactions	Main effects are clear of each other, of all 2-way interactions, and of all 3-way interactions.
	1 + 4 = 5		
	2-factor Interactions	3-factor interactions and higher-order interactions	Two-way interactions are clear of each other.
	2 + 3 = 5		

- The "cost" of running fractional factorials is that effects and interactions will be confounded.
- The resolution (indicated by the Roman numeral) describes the degree of confounding; the higher the number, the more resolution (= less confounding).

– A resolution V design has less confounding than a resolution III.

· Resolution tells us the type of effects that will be confounded.

SCREENING DESIGNS

· They study the main effects of a large number of factors.

· They contain roughly the same number of runs as factors.

· They are resolution III.

· They are useful in the early stages of investigation when it is desirable to go from a large list of factors that *may* affect the response to a small list of factors that *do* affect the response.

Tips for the analysis of screening designs —

· Check the confounding results carefully.

· An important effect labeled C, for example, could also be the result of several 2-factor interactions.

· Analyze the collapsed design.

· If only factors A, F, and G turn out to be important, drop the other factors and analyze the design again.

PLACKETT-BURMAN DESIGNS

· Such designs follow a special pattern of confounding to let you reduce the number of runs needed.

· Plackett-Burman designs are available for $4(i)$ runs where i is an integer.

	Runs									
Factorial Screening Design	4	8	16			32				
Plackett-Burman Design			12		20	24	28		36	40	44

When to use Plackett-Burman Designs
- Use them when it is too costly to run the 2k (8-, 16-, or 32-run) screening design.
- Use them only in these circumstances, because the "cost" of this design is the loss of information about where the 2-factor interactions are confounded.

Summary of fractional factorials and screening designs
- Much of the information obtained in a full factorial can be obtained using only a fraction of the full factorial.
- Screening designs can be used to screen a large number of factors in a few runs to determine which are important. In screening designs, main effects are confounded with 2-factor interactions (resolution III).
- Other fractional factorials are useful in situations where it is important to understand which factors and interactions affect the response.
- Resolution tells us which effects are confounded.
- Plackett-Burman designs can be used in screening situations where 16 or 32 runs are too costly.

FULL FACTORIALS WITH MORE THAN TWO LEVELS

Full Factorial Designs can be constructed for any number of factors with any number of levels. When there are more than two levels, they provide all the benefits of the Factorial designs, as well as the Response Surface Designs.

Full Factorial Designs often have many runs. For example, a design with —

> 1 factor at 2 levels
>
> 1 factor at 3 levels
>
> 1 factor at 5 levels

— has 30 runs.

This design is particularly useful when you want to study a factor that it is difficult to represent with 2 levels. For example, if there are multiple ovens used in production, you may want to understand the behavior of all of them, not just two of them.

Planning and preparing for a Designed Experiment
Before the Experiment:
- A. Preliminaries
- B. Identifying responses, factors and factor levels
- C. Selecting the design

During the Experiment:
- D. Collecting the data

After the Experiment:
- E. Analyzing the data
- F. Drawing, verifying, and reporting conclusions
- G. Implementing recommendations

COMPLETION CHECKLIST

By the end of Phase 3: **Analyze**, you should be able to show your sponsor which causes you will focus on in the **Improve** Step by describing:
- · Which potential causes you identified
- · Which potential causes you decided to investigate and why
- · What data you collected to verify those causes
- · How you interpreted the data

Phase 4: IMPROVE

In Phase 4: **Improve**, you should now be ready to develop, implement, and evaluate solutions targeted at your verified cause. The goal is to demonstrate, with data, that your solutions solve the problem and lead to improvement.

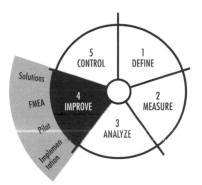

The tools most commonly used in the Improve phase are:
1. Brainstorming (covered in the Analyze phase)
2. Consensus
3. Creativity Techniques
4. Data Collection (covered in the Measure phase)
5. Design of Experiments (covered in the Analyze phase)
6. Flow Diagrams (covered in the Analyze phase)
7. FMEA (covered in the Measure phase)
8. Hypothesis Tests (covered in the Analyze phase)
9. Planning Tools
10. Stakeholder Analysis (covered in the Define phase)

GENERATING SOLUTIONS

- Review what you know about the process and the verified cause.
- Brainstorm solution ideas; use creativity techniques.
- Combine ideas into solutions.

Evaluate ideas
In order to achieve better solutions, follow these steps:
- Generate criteria
- Weight criteria
- Evaluate ideas

SOLUTION PRIORITIZATION MATRIX

Solution	Criteria and Weights					SUM
	Easy	Quick	Tech	High Impact	Customers	
	0.2	1.25	0.3	1.65	0.6	
A	3.0	10	2.4	19.8	8.4	**43.6**
B	1.2	18.75	4.2	18.15	5.4	**47.7**
C	2.6	13.75	2.7	8.25	4.8	**32.1**
D	1.2	7.5	2.7	19.8	5.4	**36.6**

(Sum of the voted ranks) X (Weight)   Highest score = best opinion overall

COST/BENEFIT ANALYSIS

- At this stage, the team has invested a lot of emotional energy into the project, however the merits of their solution may not be obvious to those outside the team.

- The team might have selected a solution that does not meet the requirements of the business.
- A formal cost/benefit analysis expresses in financial terms the implications of your solution and helps to mobilize commitment and create buy-in.
- Most organizations have their own methodology for Cost/Benefit Analysis.

ASSESSING RISKS AND PILOTING A SOLUTION

If there is an obvious winner from the evaluation step, go with that choice.

If there is no clear choice, use decision making.
- Consensus
- Majority vote
- Minority vote
- One person

Consensus

Consensus **IS NOT**:
- A unanimous vote
- Having everyone completely satisfied with the outcome
- Necessarily anyone's first choice
- Everyone getting everything they want
- Everyone finally coming around to the "right" opinion

Consensus **IS**:
- A search for the best decision through the exploration of the best of everyone's thinking
- Everyone understands the decision and can explain why it is best
- Everyone has had an opportunity to be heard

When to use consensus
The decision is...
- High impact
- High consequence
- Emotionally charged
- Full of controversy
- Wide diversity of opinion

A better decision will be made if...
- You get everyone's opinions and thoughts.
- You get full buy-in from all participants.
- You have a structured process that helps your team listen to each other.

Tips for consensus
- Use a facilitator.
- Take good notes.
- Balance power.
- Make sure there is enough time.
- Search for alternatives that meet the goals of all members.
- Encourage.
- Listen carefully. Check for understanding.
- Be open to new ideas, but don't change your mind simply to avoid conflict or speed up the decision.
- Don't just argue for your point of view.
- Seek out differences of opinion. Have people play devil's advocate.

Reducing or eliminating risks is commonly approached using FMEA. (See **Measure** Chapter.)

PILOT

Why pilot?
- To improve the solution
- To understand risks
- To validate expected results
- To smooth implementation
- To facilitate buy-in
- To identify previously unknown performance problems

When to pilot
- To confirm expected results and practicality of the solution
- To reduce the risk of failure
- The scope of change is large, and reversing the change would be difficult.
- Implementing the change will be costly.
- Changes would have far-reaching, unforeseen consequences.

Steps of a pilot program
- Select steering committees.
- Brief participants.
- Plan Pilot.
- Inform associates.
- Train employees.
- Conduct pilot.
- Evaluate results.
- Increase scope.

What is planning?
- Understand the *why*.
- Plan the work.
- Plan the tasks and the subtasks.
- Plan the time.
- Plan the people and resources.
- Understand if it worked.

ELEMENTS OF A PLAN

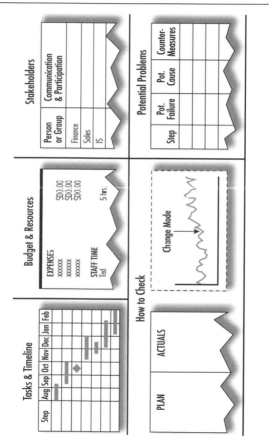

Stakeholders

Person or Group	Communication & Participation
Finance	
Sales	
IS	

Potential Problems

Step	Pot. Failure	Pot. Cause	Counter-Measures

Budget & Resources

EXPENSES
xxxxxx $0.00
xxxxxx $0.00
xxxxxx $0.00

STAFF TIME
Ted   5 hrs.

How to Check

Change Mode

PLAN	ACTUALS

Tasks & Timeline

Step	Aug	Sep	Oct	Nov	Dec	Jan	Feb

PLANNING TOOLS

TREE DIAGRAM
(See **Analyze** Chapter)

GANTT CHARTS
Gantt charts allow you to see the relationships between different tasks — such as relative sequence, duration, timing, etc. They can get complex quickly when there are many overlapping tasks. Computer software programs that automatically create Gantt charts (such as Microsoft Project) usually allow you to look at resource allocation as well as the tasks.

How to create a Gantt Chart:
1. Identify the outcome you wish to achieve. What is the last step in this process?
2. Identify the deadline for achieving this outcome.
3. Identify the first step or starting point.
4. Brainstorm all the steps in between.
5. Put them in a logical order.
6. Assign a length of time to each step.
7. Identify the nature of the relationship between steps and adjust timing if needed.
8. Label a page with appropriate time increments across the top and chart the steps.

GANTT CHART FEATURES

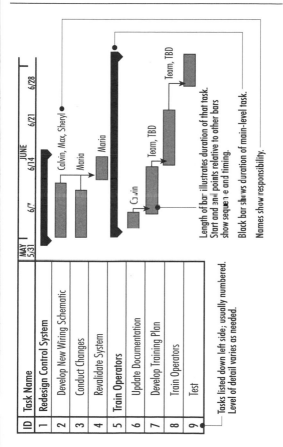

ID	Task Name
1	**Redesign Control System**
2	Develop New Wiring Schematic
3	Conduct Changes
4	Revalidate System
5	**Train Operators**
6	Update Documentation
7	Develop Training Plan
8	Train Operators
9	Test

Tasks listed down left side; usually numbered. Level of detail varies as needed.

Length of bar illustrates duration of that task. Start and end points relative to other bars show sequence and timing.

Black bar shows duration of main-level task.

Names show responsibility.

PLANNING GRID

A planning grid helps to identify the resources and outcomes for each step in the process.

How to create a planning grid

1. Specify the final outcome.
2. Identify start and ending points.
3. Brainstorm a list of steps in between.
4. Create the grid.

PLANNING GRID FEATURES

Steps listed sequentially

Outcome of each step clearly identified

Person(s) responsible identified

Timing and other factors tracked

Step Number	Step	Deliverable	Respon- sibility	Due Date	Who to Involve	Budget/ Cost	Other Topics
1	Develop new wiring schematic	Wiring Plan	Calvin, Max, Sheryl	6/2	Dept. Staff, Maria	N/A	
2	Conduct Changes	Machine Changes	Maria	6/2	Dept. Staff	N/A	
3	Revalidate System	Documentation	Maria	5/6		N/A	
4	Update Documentation	Documentation	Calvin	5/8	Other Dept. Supv.	N/A	

In addition to the above tools, the team will need to complete budget and resource planning as well as stakeholder planning.

COMPLETION CHECKLIST

By the end of Phase 4: **Improve**, you should be able to show your sponsor:

- What factors you considered to decide about the strategy
- What solutions you identified
- What criteria you used to select a solution, including how the solution was linked to the verified cause(s) identified in Phase 3: **Analyze**
- How the various alternatives scored against those criteria
- The results of any small-scale tests of the solutions
- Plans for detailed implementation
- How the planned changes align with management systems, policies, and procedures

Phase 5: CONTROL

During the **Improve** phase, the solution was piloted, and plans were made for full-scale implementation. Putting a solution in place can fix a problem for the moment, but the work in Phase 5: **Control** is designed to help you make sure the problem stays fixed and that the new methods can be further improved over time.

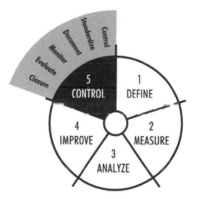

The tools most commonly used in the Control phase are:

1. Control Charts (Individuals charts and X-bar, R charts covered in the Measure phase)
2. Data Collection (covered in the Measure phase)
3. Flow Diagrams (covered in the Analyze phase)
4. Charts to compare before and after such as Frequency plots, Pareto charts, etc. (all covered in the Measure phase)
5. Quality Control Process Chart
6. Standardization

QUALITY CONTROL

To effectively maintain new standard methods, you need to:

- Verify the results and validate that changes adhere to all operating and compliance policies.

- Document the new methods in such a way that people will find them easy to use, and provide training to everyone who will use the new methods.

- Monitor implementation and make regular course corrections.

- Summarize your learnings and share them with co-workers involved in similar projects, with customers, and with managers who need to know the final outcome.

- Think about what should be tackled next in the process to further improve the sigma level.

QUALITY CONTROL PROCESS CHART

A QC Process Chart is a tool that helps you document **P**lan–**D**o–**C**heck–**A**ct (**PDCA**) for the process.

You can use any type of flowchart you want in the far left "Plan/Do" column. Typically, a deployment flowchart is used for an administrative or service process, and an activity flowchart for a manufacturing process. The key is to capture the essential steps of the process.

In manufacturing situations, the Check column will often described any technical specifications that must be met. For administrative and service process, the Check usually describes quality criteria that have been defined for the process.

An important element of Control is to make sure that everyone is using the new process according to the tested methods. These are the methods you *know* will produce desired results.

©2002 Rath & Strong/Aon Management Consulting

QC PROCESS CHART FEATURES

The plan is typically captured as a flowchart.

The middle column describes what you will check in the process to monitor its quality.

PLAN/DO	CHECK	ACT
Flowchart	Indicators	Corrective Actions
	Plot time on each order; should be ≤ 2 hours; check for special causes	Alert Sam immediately; organize investigation
	Count errors	If more than 1 per order, stop process, contact Sam

The third column describes how the process operators should react depending on what they find in the measures.

THE PLAN FOR DOING THE WORK

Flowchart	Detail on Key Tasks
Most often, people use either an activity flowchart or a deployment flowchart here.	For each key step in the operation, show how the task should be done, or provide a reference to a document that describes the step.

CHECKING THE WORK

CTQ	Monitoring Standards	Method for Recording Data
Identify in a word or phrase the characteristics to be monitored in each critical step. (e.g., elapsed time, completeness, presence of errors, or a physical characteristic such as temperature or pressure.)	For each CTQ, describe any important target, numeric limits, tolerances, or specifications to which a process should conform if it is running well. (e.g., "8 hours from receipt"; "all boxes checked"; "120° — 135° F," etc.) These standards may come from customers, regulatory policies (ISO) or process knowledge or expertise.	For each CTQ, describe how the monitored data should be recorded. (e.g., checklist, run chart, control chart, scatter plot, etc.) Describe, if necessary, who should record the data and how.

Nothing happens on a reliable, sustained basis unless we build a system to cause it to happen on a reliable, sustained basis.

ACT: THE RESPONSE TO NEGATIVE RESULTS

Damage Control	Procedure for Process Adjustment	Procedure for Systems Improvement
Who should do what with the output of the defective process? What should be done for those who received the defective output? What adjustments should be made to assure that there will be no defectives in the next iteration?	What must be done to gain sufficient under-standing of this process so that the operators know what adjustments and accommodations are routinely necessary to prevent a recurrence of this problem?	Who in the organization needs what data in what form in order to make a sound decision regarding new systems or remedies at deeper levels in the organi-zation (e.g., changes in basic designs or policies)?

STANDARDIZATION

Standardization is what allows high quality to happen on a reli-able, sustained basis.

Standardization is making sure that important elements of a process are performed consistently in the best possible way. Changes are made only when data show that a new alternative is better.

Uses for standard practices
- To reduce variation among individuals or groups (and so make process output more predictable)
- To provide "know-why" for operators and managers now on the job

- Provide a basis for training new people
- Provide a trail for tracing problems
- Provide a means to capture and retain knowledge
- Give direction in the case of unusual conditions

CREATING STANDARD PRACTICES AND PROCEDURES

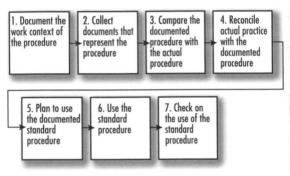

1. Document the work context of the procedure

2. Collect documents that represent the procedure

3. Compare the documented procedure with the actual procedure

4. Reconcile actual practice with the documented procedure

5. Plan to use the documented standard procedure

6. Use the standard procedure

7. Check on the use of the standard procedure

MONITORING: CONTROL CHARTS

Ongoing monitoring is typically managed with a control chart.

Uses for control charts

- Determine appropriate managerial action in response to the value of a data point from a particular process
  - To see if high or low points are due to special causes
- Understand and predict process capability (expected range of future values) for planning purposes
- Identify root causes (vital few Xs) of variation by differentiating between special and common causes of variation in the data

---

- See whether intentional changes in a process had the desired result

- Monitor key processes and identify shifts or changes quickly to help hold the gains made from an improvement project

Common-Cause Variation

Common causes are the process inputs and conditions that contribute to the regular, everyday variation in a process.

- Common causes are a part of the process.

- They contribute to output variation because they themselves vary.

- Each common cause contributes a small part of the total variation.

- By looking at a process over time, we know how much variation to expect from common causes.

- The process is stable, or predictable, when all the variation is due to common causes.

Special-Cause Variation

Special causes are factors that are not always present in a process but that appear because of some particular circumstance.

- Special causes are not usually present.

- They may come and go sporadically; may be temporary or long-term.

- A special cause is something special or specific that has a pronounced effect on the process.

- We can't predict when a special cause will occur or how it will affect the process.

- The process is unstable, or unpredictable, when special causes contribute to the variation.

Tests for Special Causes
- 8 or more points in a row on the same side of the median indicates a process shift.
- If the data are symmetrical, it's OK to use the average as the centerline instead of the median.
- 6 or more points in a row continuously increasing or decreasing indicates a trend.
- Start counting at the point where the direction changes.
- Too few runs indicates a shift in the process average, a cycle, or a trend.
- Too many runs indicates sampling from two sources, over-compensation, or a bias.
- 14 or more points in a row alternating up and down indicates bias or sampling problems.
- One or more points outside the control limits indicates that something is different about those points.

Individuals Chart — Because they can be used with any data that is time-ordered, and in general are very versatile, individuals charts are the most frequently used type of control charts. (See the **Measure** Chapter) However, with particular kinds of data or situations, they are sometimes slower to signal special causes than other kinds of charts, so it's best to understand other types of control charts as well.

SPECIFICATION LIMITS VS. CONTROL LIMITS
Specification Limits
- Come from engineering or customer requirements
- Represent what someone wants a process to do
- Can sometimes be changed by changing the requirements of the product or service

Control Limits
- Come from calculations on the process data
- Represent what a process is actually capable of doing
- Can only be changed by changing the process

When to calculate new control limits
You should calculate new control limits when
- You know there was a change in the process based on
  - Statistical evidence, such as 8 data points above or below the centerline
  - You have determined why the change occurred (based on your process knowledge).
- You are confident the process will stay changed.
  - The change was not temporary
  - The change has become a standard part of the process.

Calculate the new limits when you have enough data points to see a change. Call the new limits temporary until you get at least 24 new data points.

Assumptions for individuals charts
- Data are roughly normal (Data might need to be transformed: see **Analyze** chapter).
- Data points are independent.

What to look for when using control charts
- A good control chart is one that is being used concurrently with the process.
  - Charts should be posted or be readily at hand.
  - Charts should be up-to-date.
  - Charts should look well-used (smudged and dog-eared).

- Comments should be written on charts:
  - Dates of process changes
  - Notes on events that might cause problems later
  - Confirmation of verified special causes
  - Actions taken to eliminate special causes (only rarely should the chart indicate that the cause could not be identified)

Common Mistakes When Using Control Charts

- Chart not created correctly —
  - Wrong formula used to calculate "3 sigma" limits (st. dev. used instead of moving ranges)
  - Wrong type of chart used based on type of data collected
  - Missing, poor, or erroneous measurements
- Chart not regularly updated —
  - Data on charts are not current.
  - Process adjustments have not been noted.
  - Control limits and average have not been updated.
- Actions taken are inappropriate (or no action taken) —
  - Rewards given for "good points" or explanations sought for "bad points" even though they are not signaled as special
  - Special-cause signals ignored
  - Non-random patterns or cycles not studied to determine specific causes
  - Spec limits or goals are placed on chart instead of control limits.

CONTROL CHARTS FOR DISCRETE DATA (p, np, c, u charts)
Various control chart types

- Different types of control charts are used for different types of data.
- They all differentiate special-cause from common-cause variation.
- They all use control limits to indicate if an individual data value is due to a special cause.
- Each type of chart should have at least 24 data points to calculate control limits.

CONTROL CHARTS AND DATA TYPES
Types of Data: Recap

Continuous data is obtained by measuring.
- Examples: Seal strength, tenacity, pressure

Discrete data is obtained by counting events that meet certain criteria.
- Example: Number of damaged cartons on a pallet; number of customer complaints

p, np CHARTS

The charts are used when counting items with an attribute.

Situation 1. Equal sample sizes

Day	(n) Units Sampled/Day	(np) # of Defective Units	(p) Proportion of Defective Units
1	100	20	.20
2	100	30	.30
3	100	10	.10
•	•	•	•
•	•	•	•
•	•	•	•
•	•	•	•
•	•	•	•
24	100	20	.20

Sample sizes are all the same

np chart plots this column

p chart plots this column

Situation 2. Unequal sample sizes

Day	(n) Units Processed/Day	(np) # of Defective Units	(p) Proportion of Defective Units
1	200	20	.10
2	100	30	.30
3	300	10	.03
•	•	•	•
•	•	•	•
•	•	•	•
•	•	•	•
•	•	•	•
24	150	20	.13

Sample sizes not equal

Not appropriate to compare or plot these numbers (unequal sample sizes)

p chart plots this column; limits will change depending on n

c, u CHARTS

These charts are used when counting occurrences.

Situation 1. Equal opportunities

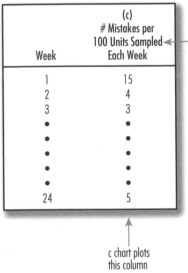

Week	(c) # Mistakes per 100 Units Sampled Each Week
1	15
2	4
3	3
•	•
•	•
•	•
•	•
•	•
24	5

There can be more than one mistake on each unit, and you cannot count the number of "non-mistakes" (so this is discrete-count data)

↑
c chart plots
this column

Situation 2. Unequal opportunities

Each unit is inspected for mistakes and most of the units are processed the first week of the month. (Area of opportunity is not the same each week.)

Week	(a) Units Processed per Week	(c) Number of Mistakes	(u) Number of Mistakes per Unit
1	104	15	.14
2	21	4	.19
3	18	3	.17
•	•	•	•
•	•	•	•
•	•	•	•
•	•	•	•
•	•	•	•
24	25	5	.20

(a) = area of opportunity; here it is not equal because we're examining each of the units processed, which varies from week to week

Not appropriate to compare or plot these numbers (c) because opportunity in not equal

u chart plots this column; (u) = (c/a) limits will change depending on (a)

CONSTRUCTING CONTROL CHARTS FOR DISCRETE DATA

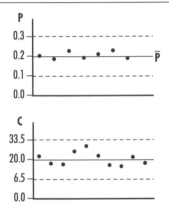

Chart	Control Limit Calculations	Distribution
p chart	$\overline{p} \pm 3 \sqrt{\dfrac{\overline{p}\,(1-\overline{p})}{n}}$	Binomial
np chart	$n\overline{p} \pm 3 \sqrt{n\overline{p}\,(1-\overline{p})}$	Binomial
c chart	$\overline{c} \pm 3\sqrt{\overline{c}}$	Poisson
u chart	$\overline{u} \pm 3 \sqrt{\dfrac{\overline{u}}{a}}$	Poisson

Assumptions of charts for discrete data

p (or np) chart assumptions are based on the binomial distribution:

- Two attributes only (e.g., defective vs. non-defective)
- The expected proportion of items with the attribute is constant (the same) for each sample.
- Occurrence of the attribute is independent from item to item.

c (or u) chart assumptions are based on the Poisson distribution:
- Can count occurrences, but not non-occurrences
- Probability of an occurrence is relatively rare (less than 10% of the time).
- Occurrences are independent (one does not influence the occurrence of another).

X-BAR, R CHARTS
These charts are used for high-volume processes with subgroups (See Measure chapter).

When to use X-bar, R charts
- Advantages over other charts:
  - Subgroups allow for a precise estimate of "local" variability.
  - Changes in process variability can be distinguished from changes in process average.
  - Small shifts in process average can be detected.

The advantages of an X, R chart disappears if systemic special causes occur — that is, a special cause that appears in each subgroup. For example, suppose you're counting errors in orders received by phone and you have four operators taking orders. It would be natural to want to construct subgroups of 4, taking one order form from each operator. But if one operator is consistently better or worse than the others, you would be mixing special-cause and common-cause variation in the data. The chart will be useless — obscuring differences between operators AND making it hard to detect changes in the process or variability.

Think carefully before you form subgroups from:

- Values from different operators, machines, shifts, fixtures
- Data determined by calendar weeks, months, or quarters

Optimal subgroup selection

In order to minimize the chance of special causes within subgroups:

- Keep subgroup size small (typically 5 or fewer data points).
- Use "adjacent" items in subgroups — made sequentially.
  - Items made or work processed "adjacent" in time will be more likely to contain only common-cause variation.

Assumption for X-bar, R Charts

Underlying assumption — common-cause variation within subgroups is equal to the common-cause variation between subgroups.

If this assumption does not hold, the X limits will either be too wide or too narrow.

EWMA CHARTS

Exponentially **W**eighted **M**oving **A**verage: These charts are used for detecting small shifts quickly. The moving average "smoothes" the variation.

EWMA charts are appropriate if:

- Data are continuous (either subgroups or individuals).
- You need to detect small shifts in the process average quickly.

- You want to be able to predict the next value in an unstable environment.
- Data need to be time ordered.

EWMA charts are not appropriate if:
- You want to identify a large sporadic special cluster (one point outside the limit).

Examples of small shifts:

Small Shifts in...	Can Have a Big Impact On...
• Interest rate	• Financials
• Percent yield	• Financials
• Market share	• Financials
• Profit margin	• Financials
• Medical instrument calibration	• Human health
• Process improvement	• Early detection of successful change

How the EWMA chart works
- Instead of weighting each point equally in the moving average, the weights decrease (exponentially) going backwards in time.
- The largest weight is given to the most recent point.
- It's like saying the chart has a memory that fades over time.
- While the calculations may seem complicated, computer software provides us with a simple way to do EWMA charts.

Current value given 20% of the weight; previous EWMA value given 80%. The first calculation uses either the historical average (in this case, "100.0") or an average of all the data.

Sequence	Output Y	Calculation	EWMA (weight 0.2)
1	78	(0.2) 78 + (0.8) 100.0	95.6
2	123	(0.2) 123 + (0.8) 95.6	101.1
3	109	(0.2) 109 + (0.8) 101.1	102.6
4	92	(0.2) 92 + (0.8) 102.7	100.5
5	105	(0.2) 105 + (0.8) 100.5	101.4
6	130	(0.2) 130 + (0.8) 101.4	107.1
7	145	(0.2) 145 + (0.8) 107.1	114.7
8	122	(0.2) 122 + (0.8) 114.7	116.2
9	150	(0.2) 150 + (0.8) 116.2	122.9
10	128	(0.2) 128 + (0.8) 122.9	123.9

The actual observations are plotted on an individuals chart

The weight of 0.2 is typical, but it can be changed

Values resulting from the EWMA calculation are plotted on an EWMA chart

SUMMARY OF CONTROL CHARTS
Procedure for using control charts

- Decide what type of control chart to use.
  - What type of data are you plotting?
  - How is it collected, individually or in subgroups?
- Construct the control chart.
- Interpret the control chart.
  - Look for signals of special causes.
  - Determine appropriate actions.
- Maintain the control chart.
  - Update the plotted points as they occur.
  - Determine appropriate actions immediately.
  - Recalculate limits when appropriate.

SELECTING A CONTROL CHART

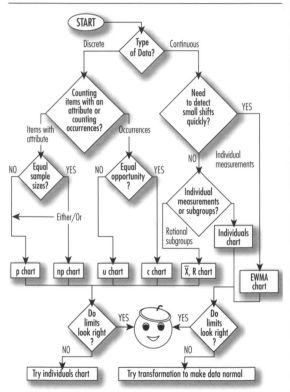

X-BAR, R CHARTS: LIMITS

Number of Observations in Subgroup (n)	Factors for $\overline{X}$ Charts		Factors for R Charts	
	$\hat{\sigma} = \overline{R}/d_2$	Control Limits: $\overline{\overline{X}} = \pm A_2\overline{R}$	Lower Control Limit: $D_3\overline{R}$	Upper Control Limit: $D_4\overline{R}$
	d_2	A_2	D_3	D_4
2	1.128	1.880	0	3.267
3	1.693	1.023	0	2.575
4	2.059	0.729	0	2.282
5	2.326	0.577	0	2.115
6	2.534	0.483	0	2.004
7	2.704	0.419	0.076	1.924
8	2.847	0.373	0.136	1.864
9	2.970	0.337	0.184	1.816
10	3.078	0.308	0.223	1.777

Situation	Chart Used	Control Limit Calculations	Comments
Counting Defects Number of defects, accidents, or flaws: # of accidents/mo. # of breakdowns/wk. # of times phone not answered within 3 rings # of flaws on an automobile	**c chart**	$\bar{c} \pm 3\sqrt{\bar{c}}$	Always plot data in time order if there is a natural chronological sequence; but may also use a **c or u chart** on non-time-ordered data such as when comparing facilities. **Notation: c** is the count of occurrences; **c̄** is the average.
	u chart	$\bar{u} \pm 3\sqrt{\dfrac{\bar{u}}{a}}$	Use when the area of opportunity varies; that is, if the size of the area or population at risk changes. **Examples:** reorganization doubles the number of employees in one division, doubling the area of risk; different automobiles have different-size hoods, so areas where scratches can occur varies. **Notation: u = c/a,** plus **a = area of opportunity.**
Fraction of "defectives" Fraction of requests not processed within 15 min.	**p chart**	$\bar{p} \pm 3\sqrt{\dfrac{\bar{p}\,(1-\bar{p})}{n}}$	**Notation:** **n = the number of units per subgroup** **x = the number of units found defective** **p = the proportion of defectives (= x/n)**
Fractions of requests not processed perfectly the first time through (first-pass yield)	**np chart**	$n\bar{p} \pm 3\sqrt{n\bar{p}\,(1-\bar{p})}$	The **np chart** is usable when **n is roughly constant.** For **p or np charts,** the fraction must be based on counts, not measurements (for proportions of measurements, use an **individuals chart**). E.g., for proportion of labor cost to total cost (both costs are continuous measurements, not counts), use an **individuals chart.**

Situation	Chart Used	Control Limit Calculations	Comments
Variables data, one figure at a time Sales, costs, variances, customer satisfaction score, total	**Individuals chart**	$\overline{X} \pm 2.66\overline{R}$ or $\overline{X} \pm 3.14\widetilde{R}$	Useable with any data over time, but not as powerful in detecting special causes as the other more specialized charts. **Note: Do not use $\overline{X} \pm 3s$** where: $s = \sqrt{\dfrac{\sum (\overline{X} - X)^2}{n-1}}$ since special causes could be masked. **Notation:** X = individual measurement, $\overline{X}$ = average $\widetilde{R}$ = median range, $\overline{R}$ = average range
Variables data, sets of measurements	**$\overline{X}$, R chart**	$\overline{\overline{X}} \pm A_2\overline{R}$ **For R chart:** UCL = $D_4\overline{R}$ LCL = $D_3\overline{R}$	Useful in, for example, measurement laboratories when the same "unknown" is measured several times per day to check measurement stability. May also be used, with care, for charts of moving averages (such as a chart of running three-month averages of customer satisfaction). **Notation:** n = number of items in subgroup (e.g., n = 3 measurements/day) X = individual measurement $\overline{X}$ = average of the subgroup $\overline{\overline{X}}$ = average of the averages $\overline{R}$ = average range of values in the subgroup

SUMMARY OF ASSUMPTIONS FOR CONTROL CHARTS

Distribution	Related Control Charts	Assumptions
Normal distribution	Used for Individuals Charts, $\overline{X}$, R Charts, EWMA Charts	Data distributed symmetrically around a mean; peak of curve at the mean
Binomial distribution	Used for p Charts	p is constant across subgroups; occurrences are independent
Poisson distribution	Used for c Charts	Probability of occurrence is constant; occurrences are independent and rare

Display before and after data
- Add more data to an existing run chart or control chart.
- Prepare new Pareto charts for those you created.

EVALUATING RESULTS

Got acceptable results?

		YES	NO
Followed your plan?	**YES**	You did what you planned to do and got the results you wanted. Move to hand-off.	You did what you planned to do but did not get the results you wanted. Return to "cause analysis" or possibly "current situation." Study the gap. Get more data.
	NO	You got the results you wanted despite not doing what you planned to do. Determine the causes of the results — what did you unintentionally do right? Understand how to achieve good results, then move to hand-off.	You didn't do what you planned to do and got poor results. Return to "solutions." Would your initial plans solve the problems you encountered? Try again with initial plans or revise as necessary.

KEY LEARNINGS

The importance of closure
- Recognize the considerable time and effort that went into the initiative.
- Capture the learnings from the initiative.
  - About the problem or process being studied
  - About the improvement process itself
- Share the learnings.
- Hand over responsibilities for standardization and monitoring to the appropriate people.

Closure checklist:
- Avoid needless continuation
- Summarize learnings
  - About the work process
  - About the team's process

About your results
- Finalize documentation on improvements.
- Summarize future plans and recommendations.
- Communicate the ending.
- Celebrate.

COMPLETION CHECKLIST

By the end of Phase 5: **Control**, you should be able to explain to your sponsor:

- What the data showed about the effectiveness of the solution, and how the actual results compare to the plan

- Why you are now confident that the current solution should be standardized

- How the new methods have been documented and how this is used in the day-to-day business

- What you do to monitor the process and sustain the gains

- What the key learnings are and what recommendations the team developed for further improvements

Six Sigma
Publications

Don't miss these other best-selling Six Sigma publications, brought to you by Rath & Strong —

Rath & Strong's Six Sigma Pocket Guide

Rath & Strong's Six Sigma Team Pocket Guide (McGraw Hill)

Rath & Strong's Six Sigma Leadership Handbook (John Wlley & Sons)

Rath & Strong's Six Sigma/DMAIC Road Map

Rath & Strong's Lean Six Sigma Road Map

Rath & Strong's Guide to Minitab for Six Sigma: Versions 13 and 14

Rath & Strong's *Whose Fault Is It Anyway?: A Modern Fable About Six Sigma*

Time: The Next Dimension of Quality (video)

Special Discounts for Quantity Purchases.
Please call for pricing information.

FOR MORE INFORMATION, VISIT —
www.rathstrong.com

SEND E-MAIL —
rathstrong_info@aoncons.com